A NEW OWNER'S
GUIDE TO
PUGS

JG-125

Overleaf: Adult Pug owned by Cynthia Getchell.

Opposite page: Adult Pug owned by Carol G. Ayrton.

The Publisher wishes to acknowledge the following owners of the dogs in this book, including: Carole G. Ayrton, Joy Barbieri, Andrew Belmore, Anna Benedetto, Stacey Braun, Terri Castellano, Mary DiPerna, Katharine Frost, Helen Gale, Cynthia Getchell, Chantale Labelle, Nancy McCorkle, Sonja Neu, Deborah Raynor, Susan Shaw, Glory Smith, Sandra Todosychuk

The author acknowledges the contribution of Judy Iby to the following chapters: Health Care, Sport of Purebred Dogs, Identification and Finding the Lost Dog, Traveling with Your Dog, and Behavior and Canine Communication.

The portrayal of canine pet products in this book is for general instructive value only; the appearance of such products does not necessarily constitute an endorsement by the authors, the publisher, or the owners of the dogs portrayed in this book.

Printed and Distributed by T.F.H. Publications, Inc.
Neptune City, NJ

A New Owner's
Guide to
PUGS

Sonja Neu and
Richard G. Beauchamp

T.F.H. Publications, Inc.
One TFH Plaza
Third and Union Avenues
Neptune City, NJ 07753

This book has been published with the intent to provide accurate and authoritative information in regard to the subject matter within. While every precaution has been taken in preparation of this book, the publisher and author assume no responsibility for errors or omissions. Neither is any liability assumed for damages resulting from the use of the information herein.

ISBN 0-7938-2774-4

Printed and bound in the United States of America

Contents

2001 Edition

Providing your Pug with a stable environment will benefit him greatly.

Pugs have the ability to make friends easily, and they enjoy the company of other pets.

With the proper training, the Pug can achieve any goal he desires.

The Pug's wide-eyed, gentle expression is his most endearing characteristic.

The amiable and good-natured Pug is an ideal companion for people of all ages.

The Pug's sensitive and affectionate nature makes him a wonderful companion for people of all ages.

THE ESSENCE OF THE PUG

A Delightful Companion

The Pug is a pleasure to live with and a delight to own. The most endearing quality of the Pug is his desire to be your loyal friend and loving companion. A Toy breed, the Pug is compact, alert, and happy being by his master's side. He appears in two colors: fawn and black, with the fawn varying from light to dark. Despite the coat color, the Pug always has a black mask and muzzle. The black color usually has no other markings.

The Pug adapts easily to his living environment, whether it is in a small apartment in the city or in a large, open home in the country. However, he does not prefer to live in a kennel- or basement-like area that is separate from his loved ones. The Pug wants and needs to be an integral part of his family's life.

The Pug is an adopted spirit child that has the uncanny ability to sense your feelings. A perceptive breed, the Pug will try to comfort you when he senses that you are upset. He is understanding when you are sad. He is a court jester when you are happy. He is at your feet when you are busy. A one-family dog, the Pug makes it his business to know his family's habits, desires, and idiosyncrasies.

Self-assured and attentive, the Pug is always by your side. If you are watching your favorite television program, the Pug will be stretched out beside you or in someone else's lap waiting for the commercial-break treat. He will follow you everywhere, even to the bathroom, and wait persistently by the door. He will sleep and cuddle with you, if you allow him to do so. The Pug is protective of his family and will do his best to warn his people of an intruder. A Pug will have affection for all of his family members, but will demand the attention from the one who feeds him and pays the most attention to him. Some Pugs, when greeting an individual, will ever so gently nibble or lick the new acquaintance's fingertips. A few breeders suggest that a Pug's taste is keener than his smell and that tasting is his way of imprinting that person's mannerisms.

The Charmer

The Pug abounds with charm and dignity, which causes him to

As one of the most animated breeds of dog, the Pug is a true entertainer that enjoys acting out his owner's whims.

be a clown one minute and a crowned prince the next. He is sensitive, well mannered, playful, demanding, and intelligent. He is capable of communicating with his dark, round eyes and knows what you expect of him without a word spoken.

It's a Pug's greatest pleasure to please his master. He is sensitive to neglect and harsh punishment, but he can handle a firm correction well. If he wants your attention, he will figure out a method to obtain it. The Pug loves to travel by car, train, plane, bike, wagon, or even in a child's stroller; any form of transportation will do. He is proud to escort you anywhere at anytime. He adores children and is sensitive to their size, knowing when to play gently with a small child and more assertively with an older child. Some Pugs love to play "dress up," and will display an extra air of radiant attitude when wearing a special outfit, such as a satin ribbon or handsome bow tie.

Cleanliness is a definite trait in the breed, which makes owning a Pug a pleasure. It is not unusual to view a Pug washing his face with his front paws, occasionally purring. He does not like to be dirty and enjoys his bath time. For Pugs, cleanliness is a priority, so paper training your Pug is easy. This potty-training method is a saving device for anyone who lives in the city or experiences inclement weather. The male Pug tends to be boyish in his attitude and enjoys frolicking in the rain, while the female is a bit more prissy and definitely does not want to get her soft hair wet. When it's pouring outside, the Pug will usually give you that "no way" expression, ignoring you until you get the umbrella and rain gear.

The Pug is a low-impact exerciser and enjoys a brisk evening or morning stroll during the cool hours. He is capable of taking a short hike to the lake or through the woods, chasing rabbits, or being a little sportsman. Be prepared—he will expect you to carry a cold water bottle for his refreshment when he desires it. A Pug loves being pampered and returns the love tenfold. He is not a dog that can be chained in the backyard; however, he needs the safety of a fenced area to roam. Most top show Pugs are road worked or walked on a treadmill one to three miles a day to keep their muscles in firm, hard condition. However, the greatest enjoyment for a Pug is watching you exercise while he plays with a soft overstuffed toy.

THE PUG'S CURIOUS NATURE

Many unique traits have helped endear the Pug to his owner. He loves stretching out on a high spot or resting on the back of the sofa. He will search for a window that will let him view what is happening in the neighborhood while he suns himself. Whereas curiosity gets the cat in trouble, it amuses the Pug.

Despite the Pug's thick build, he is agile and finds agility a great sport in which to participate. He can be enthusiastic and

It's not unusual to catch your Pug taking a midday breather. The Pug's leisure time is essential to his peace of mind and well-being.

as proud as a peacock over his accomplishments. The Pug has an above-average intelligence; he wants to know what is going on at all times. He easily learns the daily behaviors that are demanded of him by his owner and responds well to formal training. However, a Pug will try to spice up his practice sessions if boredom sets in from repetition. A trainer needs to have patience to overcome the Pug's antics and will have to be one step ahead of him at all times during training. A Pug can have you under his spell quite easily. He can and will find solutions to problems, such as how to get from one place to another when an obstacle is in his way.

A STABLE TEMPERAMENT

The Pug is known for his stable temperament. Through socialization with his breeder and owner, the Pug's characteristics become more fully developed. He is not high-strung but has the poise to usher you anywhere. He is polite with strangers and dedicated to his owner. He easily adapts to a new home and readily accepts a kind master. Many rescue Pugs who have been abused or neglected are thankful to receive a new home and will want to please and love their kind family.

The Pug's gentle and comedic nature helps put other pets at ease. Labl's Miagy-Oko and De/Enclo's Lucky Charm Labl's prove that friends come in all shapes and sizes.

Although the Pug is a hardy eater and looks forward to his meals, do not let his appetite exceed a healthy limit.

The Pug is known for his loyalty and will grieve a loss of a family member. He displays many emotions and loves the comforts of a home, the softness of a lap, and a box of toys. A Pug ages with dignity and charm and on an average, lives to the age of 12. Other pets will enjoy the comical presence of a Pug. He is a comfort, a heart snatcher, a one-act comedian, a gentleman, and best of all, a true and loving companion.

BREED EXPECTATIONS

Anyone interested in owning a Pug might ask if there are any problems associated with the breed. Most breeds have complications or breed characteristics that others might not appreciate, but this compact character will win your heart. The Pug is a hardy eater and thoroughly enjoys his meals and his treats. However, if your Pug becomes sluggish and overweight, then it is time for a diet. The Pug's body should be in proportion; when looking down over his back, the front should be as wide as the rear.

Shedding does occur in the breed. The Pug's soft hair can attach to any material, but his short coat causes few allergies. Major shedding takes place twice a year—once in the spring and then in the fall. Both colors of Pugs shed and need to be fed an excellent quality food with the addition of amino fatty acids to help retard shedding and to keep the coat in the best possible condition.

Pugs can receive eye injuries. Twigs and other objects can get in their eyes; therefore, an owner needs to keep hard, low-growing branches trimmed, be aware of thorns on bushes, and mow tall grass and weeds. If there is a cat or another animal in the household, make sure that all encounters are supervised.

Snoring is common in Pugs, which many owners feel has a soothing effect. Pugs have a tendency to sneeze on anything and to twitch their noses. They usually don't like to have their toenails shortened, even when they are a few weeks old. They will sit on your feet when you are talking on the phone or when you are visiting with your neighbor. Many will even try to talk to you by puckering their lips and making little "woo" noises.

It is important to obtain a Pug that was raised in a caring home and not in a kennel. A Pug raised in a home-like atmosphere will adjust quickly, have more personality, and automatically tune in to your lifestyle. He will not be scared of a vacuum cleaner or a dishwasher, and he will know how to climb steps. A Pug can be assertive or bold, but not aggressive; however, he will defend himself when necessary. Pugs love attention and would be happy going for a walk in the park, sitting on the bench at a restaurant, or watching the kids play baseball. If you neglect your Pug, he will spend most of his time trying to get your attention.

Providing your Pug with a loving and caring environment will increase his longevity and help him to become a well-adjusted and obedient companion.

Although the Pug enjoys the outdoors, he cannot exist solely outside. He is a companion lap dog. He is also brachycephalic and can overheat quickly, which could lead to death. No one should obtain a Pug if they intend to have him as an outside pet. A Pug needs a home that is heated in the winter, air conditioned in the summer, and full of caring love.

Although many Pug breeders believe that the black Pug is more intelligent and independent than the fawn-colored Pug, there aren't any major character differences between them. In fact, both black and fawn

Despite what some Pug breeders believe, there are no major differences between the black Pug and the fawn Pug. They both have stable temperaments and good senses of humor.

can be born of two fawn parents. The temperament is stable in both colors, and both colors will entertain you. Whether black or fawn, the Pug is comedic, curious, even-tempered, and entertaining; each Pug has his own unique personality.

The Pug is the perfect breed for levelheaded people that want a sturdy, devoted pet with personality and not an obedient machine. Although the Pug is energetic and enthusiastic, he is never rowdy. He enjoys being with other animals, entertaining small children, and visiting with the elderly. He has the ability to sense when something is wrong. The Pug is capable of establishing a meaningful relationship with his master based on a mutual understanding. The Pug is a charmer, complete with a keen curiosity and a stable temperament. Today's Pug breeders have made great efforts to keep the Pug a special package that will be your loyal friend and companion for a lifetime.

A LONG JOURNEY

ANCIENT CHINESE LO-CHIANG DOG

In ancient Chinese documents, it is recorded that short-mouthed dogs existed in China during the time of Confucius, which was around 700 BC. Two hundred years later, the Chinese wrote that dogs were used for sporting purposes in the Province of Shansi. V.W.F. Collier states in his book, *Dogs of China and Japan in Nature and Art*, "Some of these were probably small dogs, for it is mentioned that after the day's sport, one kind of dog followed its master's chariot, while those having short mouths were carried in the carts."

In ancient China, all treasures, including pearls, jade, dogs, or rare animals, were considered imperial property. About 1 AD the word "pai" came into use in China, referring to a small dog that has short legs and a short head. Emperor Ling To (168-190 AD) reared pai dogs and gave them rank, with the females receiving the same rank as his wives. These dogs were guarded by soldiers

About 1 AD, the Chinese word "pai" came into use, referring to a small dog that has short legs and a short head.

According to the Chinese, the wrinkles on the forehead of a short-mouthed dog, known as prince characters, were of great value.

and fed the best rice and meat. If anyone attempted to steal them, he or she would be sentenced to death.

Around 900 AD, the word *lo-chiang-sze* was used in the Peking area to describe a small dog that has short legs, a short head, and short hair. *Lo-chiang-sze* was shortened to *lo-chiang* and later to *lo-sze*. The word *lo-chiang* is important because it is the first mention of coat length, which allowed people to differentiate the Pug from the Pekingese.

A famous poet named Li Chih wrote long odes in honor of a little lo-chiang dog named T'oa Hua:

"About the year 990 A.D., an official in Ssuchuan gave the Emperor T'ai Tsunh of the Sung Dynasty a lo-chiang dog named T'oa Hua (peach flower) from Ho-Chow (about fifty miles north of Chungking). It was extremely small and very intelligent. It followed the Emperor everywhere. When there was an audience, the dog preceded him, and by its bark announced its imperial master's arrival. When the Emperor T'ai Tsunh was ill, the dog refused to eat. When the Emperor died, the dog manifested its sorrow with tears and whining. The palace eunuchs endeavored to train the dog to precede the new Emperor, but without success. The Emperor had made an iron cage with white cushions in sign of mourning, and this, containing the dog, was carried in the imperial chair to his master's tomb. There, the dog died, and the Emperor Chen Tsung (a faithful disciple true to the Confucian doctrine) issued a decree ordering it to be wrapped in the cloth of an imperial umbrella and buried alongside of its master."

The Chinese placed considerable importance on superstitions regarding the color and markings bred in dogs. To the Chinese, every color and every marking served to crystallize some superstitious thought. Symmetrical markings, known as prince characters, wrinkled on the forehead of a short-mouthed dog were of great value. Sometimes, the Chinese docked the dogs' tails for a symmetrical form. However, the curly tail *(sze kuo chu-erh)* and the double curl tail were also known to have existed.

Breeding to closely defined points and adhering to the pedigree standards was never done in China. The only recognizable standards to which dogs were bred are those contained in the dog books of each imperial master, as illustrated by the court painter. Each emperor had illustrations of his favorite dogs made on scrolls or in books, which set the fashion in breeding.

THE SPIRIT LION AND THE LO-SZE PUG

The Chinese were greatly influenced by superstitious ideas and religious values in the breeding of their dogs. They actually bred for a likeness between the spirit lion and the Pug, the *lo-sze*. In China, the lion came alive with Buddhism, which was a foreign religion that reached China directly through the Sinkian trade route, from India through Tibet. There is no doubt that the lion did not exist in China and was not a part of their natural science. The Chinese emperors of the Hans Dynasty, about 202 BC, were the first to become interested in lions. Almost 300 years later, the first importation of lions occurred around 87 AD Many of the emperors look upon the lion with intense admiration. However, the lion spirit statue never resembled a true lion specimen because few Chinese artists ever had the opportunity to view a real lion. In China, the figure of a spirit lion is frequently used as a charm, which is placed at the front of a door.

Buddhism flourished until Genghis Khan conquered Tibet in 1206 and introduced Lamaism. Lama priests distinguished a

Superstition played a large role in the Pug's origin. The Chinese actually bred the Pug to resemble the revered lion spirit.

difference between their spiritual beast, the true lion, whose images are capable of infinite magnification or reduction in size, and the dog lions that are found in Buddhist sacred places. The Lamaists teach that the dog lion is inferior to the true lion of their religion. However, the Buddhists revered dogs and held the Chinese Toy dogs sacred, based on the likeness between the idolized statue and the dog. Both the Tibetans and the Chinese bred a race of Toy dogs to resemble their ideal spirit lion.

The following Buddhist gospels help to explain the Chinese's interest in breeding Toy dogs that resembled their lion spirit:

"In the West, there was a Buddha named Wenshu who was always accompanied by a small hah-pah (pet) dog and who traveled the four continents as a simple priest. On his travels, he one day met a Taoist who begged him to obtain an audience with Manjusri. The Buddha invited the Taoist to accompany him to his home. When the Taoist had taken tea and rice, he again requested the Buddha to secure for him a vision of Manjusri Buddha. The Buddha told him that he must observe his vows with great strictness and that Manjusri would then be manifested to him. On this, the Taoist, bursting into anger, cried vehemently, 'I am indeed keeping my vows. If not, why should I have come hither conquered by a small hah-pah (pet) dog and who traveled the four continents as a simple priest.' Then said the Buddha, 'If this be verily so, look up into the sky.' The Taoist raised his head and perceived in the sky a glow of five-colored lights together with clouds of five colors. In the heavens, he saw the hah-pah dog transformed into a mighty lion with the Buddha riding upon his back.

"The lion of the King of Beasts. Its power of increase is without limit. Similarly, it may diminish at will and become like unto a dog."

The Chinese held the lo-sze dogs that resembled the lion in the highest esteem. The lion spirit simulates a short-muzzle dog more than a cat, which is the monarch of the jungle. It is said that spinning together hair from a dog and hair from a lion is a magical prescription against sickness.

ALWAYS IN VOGUE

V.W. F. Collier states, "It was very possible the Chinese Pug appears to have been fashionable at the Chinese court from the beginning of the 8th century to the middle of the 11th century— possibly even to the removal of the capital from Hsianfu to

Peking, about 1153 AD" During the Yuan Dynasty (1206-1333), there are two references to the "golden-coated dog," also called "nimble dog," that was commonly bred by people in their own homes. During feasts, it was customary to parade all the emperor's animals in front of his impressed guests. The golden-coated, nimble dogs that were small and short in body were presented after the lions. It is believed that these dogs were introduced to Europe at this time.

For the next 300 years, during the Ming Dynasty (1368-1628), the Chinese, with their super-stitious values, were more interested in breeding cats, even though the adored lo-sze dogs had served the Chinese for centuries. However, during the Middle Ages, cats were in fashion, persuading people with their magical influence. The Dutch were trading in the Orient in the early part of the 16th century and established a factory at Firando before 1600. We know that the Pug existed in other parts of the world at this time, but the Dutch cherished the Pug, and their artwork gives us a more factorial background for the breed. There is no doubt that the Pug in Japan and the Chinese pai dog became dear to the ladies in Japan. "Wo Tzu" became the Japanese word for the Chinese pai dog. During this time, Pugs were imported to Russia and Spain.

The black Pug has enjoyed notoriety in past centuries. In 1653, Dutch artist Q. Brekelenham painted The Tailor's Shop, *one of the first paintings that included a black Pug.*

The "Light-Colour'd Dutch Dog"

Without question, the Pug was a recognizable breed in Holland. In 1572, the King of Holland, William the Silent, took his Pugs with him when he waged war against the Spanish. Miraculously, one of William's Pugs awakened him in time to save him from assassination. One hundred years later, the Dutch Pug crossed the English Channel when King William's son, Prince William, ascended the throne in England. Prince William appeared with his regal Pugs that were adorned with orange ribbons, and a year later, his wife, Mary II, arrived with her Pugs that also wore orange ribbons in honor of the House of Orange.

In 1653, Dutch artist Q. Brekelenham painted *The Tailor's Shop,* which displays a black Pug—one of the first paintings done of a black Pug in Europe. This great work was completed 77 years before Hogarth, the famous painter from Holland, created the painting titled *The House of Cards,* which depicts a black Pug in the year 1730. These paintings prove that black Pugs were in Holland 150 years before Lady Brassey returned to England from her voyage to China with black Pugs. The Pug was a trademark to Hogarth, as the lion was a trademark to Leonardo da Vinci. Hogarth had several Pugs in his lifetime. One of his Pugs became lost, and Mr. Hogarth advertised in *The Craftsman Newspaper* on December 5, 1730, offering a reward for this "light-colour'd Dutch dog with a black muzzle and answers to the name Pugg." Later, Hogarth carved the following epitaph to one of his dead Pugs: "Life to the last enjoyed, here Pompey lies."

In Hogarth's self portrait, which hangs in the Tate Gallery in London, a Pug named Trump sits next to the artist. Louis Francois Roubiliac also did a sculpture of Hogarth and Trump, which can be viewed at the Victoria and Albert Museum in London.

Around 1736, the Pug played a small part in German history. After the Masons were excommunicated by the Pope, the Pug became their secret symbol and the Freemasons' order became known as the "Mopsorden" or the "Order of the Pug." The Mopsorden was led by the Grand Master of the Freemasons, the Elector of Saxony, who was the most important patron of the Meissen factory. Lovely porcelain Pug figurines were produced by the Meissen factory under the supervision of Count Bruhl, the managing director, who had several Pugs of his own. The figurines were likely examples of his numerous Pugs and display the Pug type of the era. The Pugs' ears were cropped and they wore collars with bells or lockets.

Because the Pug was supposedly crossbred with so many other types of dog, Pug breeders have diligently tried to breed back to the original Chinese type.

In Goya's 1785 painting, *La Marquesa de Pontejos*, a splendid female Pug full of the personality and type that was popular in Spain is depicted. This painting was done 50 years after the production of the Meissen figurines, and this little darling's ears are not cropped, but she is wearing the collar with bells.

THE DRAGON-CLAW PUG

V.W. F. Collier states in *Dogs of China and Japan in Nature and Art,* "The most admired and rarest of the breed was the *loong chua lo-sze* (dragon-claw Pug), which was short-coated except for the ears, the toes, behind the legs, and the chrysanthemum-flower tail, all of which were very well feathered. This appears to have been a distinct race, which became extinct about 50 years ago (1875). The Pug-dog occurred in any color, and was bred as small as possible." This is possibly the best representation of the Chinese lion spirit.

NOT A BABY BULLDOG

Many past authors have stated that Pugs derived from the Bulldog or the Mastiff; however, ancient Chinese writings and studies of the breed's bone remains conclude that this is not true. In 1867, the Zoological Society stated that it is impossible to distinguish a difference in the oriental breed skulls of the Pug and the Pekingese. However, there are radical differences between the Pug's skull and the Bulldog's or the Mastiff's skull.

In 1859, J. H. Walsh complained about using the Pug for crossbreeding. "The Pug, the only naturally known short-faced dog in Europe at that time, was used in crossbreeding to shorten the muzzles of other canine types," Walsh stated. Sydenham Teak Edwards tells us in his *Cynographia Britannica* (1800) that Pugs were previously crossed with Bulldogs to shorten the faces of the latter. Veldhuis, a woman who studied old German and Dutch dogs, states that the Pug was crossbred to the old German Pinscher to achieve the shorter face of the German Pinscher in the 18th century. The Pug was also crossbred to terriers and possibly left his mark on multiple breeds in Europe. Many of the Pug breeders wanted to keep the Pugs pure and therefore bred back to the original Chinese type, which is why so much importance has been placed on Click, the pure Chinese fawn Pug, and Jack Spratt, the pure Chinese black Pug.

CLICK, PURE CHINESE STOCK

James Watson, author of *The Dog Book*, states "...as far back as we can distinguish between what the Chinese meant to be a dog and what were the dog of Fo (Japan), we find the pug-headed, curled-tailed dog that was the progenitor of the Pekingese dog. There is no way getting away from the obvious, the very plain indication that the Pug was an oriental importation. Even if that was not the actual origin of the Pug, we owe a great deal to the smooth Pekingese, as nearly all our Pugs trace back to one particular cross of the dog from China. All the English Pugs of prominence from 1865 to 1895, also the best Pugs from 1880 to 1900, can be traced back to Click, a dog of pure Chinese stock."

Mrs. Laura Mayhew of Twickenham, London, was the prominent owner of Click. Her son, Reginald Mayhew, gave the following account of his mother's Pugs and of the breeders in the late 1800s: "At the outset the winning English Pugs were of Dutch origin, and among the chief breeders were my mother and Mr. Morrison, the latter being landlord of an old-fashioned roadhouse, in the outskirts of Chelsea. In those days, Pugs were cropped and in general type were tight-skinned, straight faced, apricot fawn in color, and as a rule had good, wide set eyes, which gave them a fairly good expression."

A few years afterward, in the late 1860s, Lord Willoughby became a prominent factor in Pugdom, so much that the term "Willoughby Pug" was as common an expression in the breed as "Laverack setter" was in English Setters. Lord Willoughby obtained his original specimens from a tight-rope walker known as the female Blondin, who brought them from St. Petersburg. They were silver fawns, the majority being smutty in color, with pinched faces and small eyes, but better wrinkled than the Dutchmen.

Reverting to their color, I have seen so many born practically black (smutty) in those old days and consigned to the bucket on that account, that I have to consider the introduction of the black Pug a novelty. In fact, when Lady Brassey introduced the black variety, her specimens had the inherent faults of the Willoughby stain—pinched faces, small eyes, legginess, and tight skins. In fact, the only really good-headed black Pug I have seen here (New York) was Mrs. Howard Gould's Black Knight.

Still, the winning specimens, typical as they were, lacked that grandeur in head that the ideal called for. It wasn't until my

The Pug's grand skull, large round eyes, square muzzle, and short face can be traced to Click, the famous Chinese Pug.

mother became the owner of Click that grand heads and beautiful expressions were seen on the bench. Click has long been a household name in Pugdom; the best winners from the past 25 years have been traced back to him. In fact, all the grand skulls, big appealing eyes, square muzzles, and short faces are due to Click.

As for Click himself, he was an apricot fawn, with an ideal head and expression and the most beautiful eyes. He was rather narrow behind and as rough in coat as Mrs. Gould's Black Knight, which, if you altered his color, would be a very good sample of Click.

Click's parents, Lamb and Moss, were Chinese beyond dispute. They were captured in the Emperor of China's palace during the siege of Peking in 1867 or 1868 and were brought to England by the Marquis of Wellesley. They were given to Mrs. St. John. Alike as two peas, they were solid apricot fawn, without a suspicion of white, and had lovely heads and expressions; however, unlike their son, they were close to the ground and a little lengthy in body. The pair was so much alike that my mother firmly believed that they were brother and sister.

I cannot leave the Pug subject without expressing regret that popular feeling tends to hold the breed in a ridiculous light. No breed in its specimens has such distinct individuality. In character, the Pug is intelligent, consequential to a degree, willing to take his own part, and outgoing. Being short-coated, Pugs do not require half the attention called for by the more popular variety of Toys, such as Pomeranians, Spaniels, and Yorkshire Terriers, while they are more robust in constitution and of a more independent spirit.

Click, the direct descendent of the Chinese Lamb and Moss, is the major contributor to the best show Pugs in England and in America. Dr. Cryer's book, *Prize Pugs of America and England*, shows that about 50 percent of the leading winning Pugs in America are from Click crosses.

FIRST GENERATION OF THE AMERICAN PUG

James Watson reported that the first Pug of quality in this country was Dr. Cryer's Roderick, a dog of correct size but handicapped by very straight hind legs to the extent of being double-jointed. It was this defect that enabled Ch. George to defeat Roderick in the majority of cases. Bred by Thomas Morris of Bolton, England, Roderick was born on July 12, 1878, and died in 1885. His sire was Champion Punch by Lord Willoughby's Jumbo and his dam was Mr. Morris's Jusy. Roderick was described as a "small dog for those days, weighing about 14 and one-half pounds. He was very good in symmetry, size, body, feet, head, ears, mask, color, and coat. The forelegs were good, but the hind legs were very weak, almost double jointed. The muzzle was fair and the eyes good, but when Roderick was two years old, each cornea became seared through keratitis. His tail was fair and his general carriage when on a carpet or smooth floor was good, but was very bad on sawdust."

Born on November 1, 1878, Ch. George was owned by Mrs. E. A. Pue from Philadelphia and bred by Lelia Tegvan of South Carolina. His sire was Muggins (pedigree unknown) and his dam was Coquette (pedigree unknown). Dr. Cryer described George as "always appearing at his best, as he was kept in fine condition, body, legs, feet, mask, wrinkles, trace, coat, and neck he was fair.

His eyes were large and expressive, but too light in color. His ears were not good in shape, nor well carried, and he was over size, nearly twenty-five pounds."

Another Pug that cannot be forgotten is Ch. Joe, an import from England where he was known as Zulu II. Born on March 31, 1879, and bred by Mrs. Jameson of Middlesborough, Ch. Joe was owned by George Hill from Maderia, Ohio. Joe is also a descendant of Click and beat the best dogs of his time. In 1883, a young man brought Joe to America for Mrs. Jameson. When the young man got to New York, he left the dog in payment of his board bill. The owner of the boarding house sent word to Mr. Mortimer, a dog judge who lived in Pittsburgh, that he had a Pug dog he wanted to sell. Mr. Mortimer went to view this Pug, paid the amount, and took him home. Surely he was quite happy with his find and traced the dog to his owner in England. In 1884, Joe won seven championship prizes out of eight and was described as one of the best Pugs in America, having beaten all the best.

Of the bitches in the 1880s, the best were Mr. Knight's Effie and Dr. Cryer's imported Dolly. Effie was born on May 24, 1880, and was bred by Mrs. S. Collingswood. Her sire was G. H. Foster's Banjo and her dam was Zoe, down from Click. She was a top-winning bitch, but unfortunately, was not able to reproduce. However, Cryer's Dolly produced Max, Bessie, and Dude, whose son was named Bob Ivy and called "Little Bob." Bob Ivy was a correct little dog in every way, and his size was all one could desire.

Bessie was born on April 6, 1885 and was owned and bred by Dr. Cryer. Bessie is described as small, clear, and right in color everywhere except in the nails, well built, tight in twist, excellent in wrinkle and skull, and irresistible in eyes. Bessie's sire was Othello, whose color was smutty throughout, but Dr. Cryer stated that he would rather breed a small bitch to Othello than to any other dog he knew. Later, Bessie, who was bred in America, was taken back to England to compete, where she did win.

Another great bitch of the time was Ch. Bo-Peep, the first of the American-bred Pugs to win a championship. She died in a dreadful fire in Columbus, Ohio, on January 12, 1888. Ch. Bo-Peep was bred by A. W. Lucy of New York and was owned by Mr. H. L. Goodman.

The improvement in the Pugs in America continued each year through the helpful hands of Miss Annie Whitney, Massachusetts; Walter Peck, Connecticut; Forest City Kennels, Maine; Harry Goodman, Illinois; Mrs. Wheatley, New York; Miss Bannister,

Thanks to the dedication and knowledge of Pug breeders throughout history, the Pug has continued to improve and succeed.

New Jersey; the Messers, the Gillivans, the Pitts, and the Eberharts, Ohio; Mr. Hudson, Michigan; the Acme Kennels of Milwaukee; and the Fishers and Cryers, Pennsylvania. Their goals were to breed American Pugs that could win on the other side of the Atlantic and to continue to improve on the quality that they now possess.

CHRONOLOGICAL HISTORY OF THE PUG

700 BC
· In China, short-mouthed dogs existed in the time of Confucius.
· The *Book of Rites* stated that "dogs are of three kinds: hunting dogs, watch dogs, and those used for culinary purposes."

500 BC
· It is recorded in ancient writings that dogs were used for sporting purposes in the Province of Shansi. "Some of these were probably small dogs, for it is mentioned that after the day's sport, one kind of dog followed its master's chariot, while those having short mouths were carried in the carts."

1 AD
· During this time, the Chinese books became a little more specific, speaking of a "pai" dog, which refers to a very small short-legged and short-headed type of dog.

700-1153
• V.W.F. Collier wrote, "It was very possible the Chinese Pug appears to have been fashionable at the Chinese court from the beginning of the eighth century to the middle of the eleventh century—possibly even to the removal of the capital from Hsisnfu to Peking, about 1153 AD."

824
• Japan's emperor demanded that the Chinese government pay tribute to him by giving him two pai dogs.

900
• The word *lo chiang-sze* was the original name for the short-haired Pug. It was then shortened to the word *lo-sze*. "It therefore appears possible that the lo-chiang dog, so famous in Chinese history, was in reality practically identical with the English Pug, which is known to have descended from Chinese ancestors." The lo-chiang dog was likely the pai dog before 900 AD.

990
• Emperor T'ai Tsunh of the Sung Dynasty was given a lo-chiang dog named T'ao Hua (peach flower). This dog followed the emperor everywhere. When there was an audience, the dog preceded him, and by her bark announced her master's arrival. When the emperor died, the dog manifested her sorrow with tears and whining. T'ao hua died at her master's tomb.

1206-1333
• During the Yuan Dynasty, it was customary to parade all the emperor's animals in front of his guests. After the lions, dogs that were small and short in body called "golden-coated nimble dogs" were presented. It is possible that these dogs were introduced to Europe at this time.

1368-1628
• During the Ming Dynasty, the Chinese turned their efforts to cat breeding. It is suspected that the Chinese preferred the cat over the dog during the Middle Ages because of the cat's association with witchcraft and other superstitions.

1572
• The King of Holland, William the Silent, took his Pugs along with him when he waged war against the Spanish. At Hermigny, he was awakened by one of his Pugs just in time to avoid being assassinated.

1653

Lo-chiang-sze *was the original name for the short-haired Pug. The lo-chiang dog that was so famous in Chinese history was practically identical to the English Pug.*

• Dutch artist Q. Brekelenham painted *The Sailor's Shop*, which includes a black Pug. This is one of the first-known paintings of a black Pug.

1686-1766

• Chinese artist Tsou Yi-Kewi painted Chinese Pugs for the *Imperial Dog Book*, which includes a black lo-sze and other multi-colored lo-sze dogs.

1688

• The Pug became the official dog of the House of Orange. When Prince William traveled from Holland to England to ascend his throne, Pugs attended the ceremony wearing orange ribbons. A year later, Prince William's wife, Mary II, arrived with her Pugs that also wore orange ribbons.

1728

• Gay mentions a Pug in one of his charming verses:

"Poor Pug was caught, to town conveyed,

There sold. How envied was his doom,

Made captive in a lady's room."

1730

• A painting completed by Jean-Baptiste Audrey displayed Louis XV's Pug. This masterpiece hangs in the Lille Museum of France.

• Hogarth's painting, *The House of Cards,* depicted a black Pug in Holland, which attests to the black Pugs existance there.

• Mr. Hogarth offered a reward for his lost Pug in *The Craftsman Newspaper* on December 5, 1730. The advertisement read: "light-colour'd Dutch dog, with black muzzle, and answers to the name Pugg."

1736

• Meissen's porcelain factory produced exquisite figures of Pugs. Count Bruhl, the managing director of the Meissen factory, had numerous Pugs.

• The Pug was the secret symbol of "The Order of the Pug" or the "Mopsorden" that was led by the Grand Master of the Freemasons, the Elector of Saxony. When the Pope excommunicated the Masons in Germany, they continued to function in an underground way. The Elector of Saxony was the most important patron of the Meissen factory.

1740

• Hogarth's self-portrait with his Pug, Trump, is displayed at the Tate Gallery in London. A Pug is Hogarth's trademark, as a lion was Leonardo de Vinci's.

- Louis Francois Roubiliac sculptured Hogarth and Trump, which can be seen at the Victoria and Albert Museum in London. When one of Hogarth's Pugs died, he carved an epitaph that read: "Life to the last enjoyed, here Pompey lies."
- The word "Pug-dog" was used in the play, *Lethe Aesop in the Shades*, written by Englishman David Gaarrick. "She lies in bed all morning, rattles about all day, and sits up all night...tells fibs, makes mischief, buys china, cheats at cards, keeps a Pug-dog, and hates the Parsons."
- An Italian writer who was visiting England stated that the Pug is a popular breed.

1785
- Goya painted *La Marquesa de Pontejos*, which features a dainty female Pug. This painting can be seen at the Gallery of Art in Washington, DC.

1790
- During this time, the Pug's ears were either cropped or completely cut off to give him a better facial expression.

1800
- Belgian artist Albrecht de Vriendt painted King George III playing cards. In the painting was a Pug.

1821-1851
- The cult of the lap dog reached its development.

1846
- Lord and Lady Willoughby of D'Eresby of Greenthorpe bred a Pug obtained from Vienna with a bitch brought from Holland that produced a line of Pugs with entirely dark heads and large saddlemarks. Lord Willoughby's established line produced Jumbo, a good sire, and Punch and Ch. Roderick of America.
- Mr. Morrison of Walham Green had a different strain with clearer color that descended from stock enjoyed by Queen Charlotte. The Willoughby and the Morrison Pugs were eventually bred together.

1859
- The English Stud Book was established; the first volume lists 66 Pugs.
- J. H. Walsh complained about breeders using Pugs for crossbreeding to shorten muzzles of other breeds.

1867
- The Zoological Society stated that there is a radical difference between a Pug's skull and a Bulldog's skull, but not between a Pug's and a Pekingese's skull.

1868

· During the siege of Peking, two Pugs were captured in the Palace of the Emperor. These two Pugs, named Lamb and Moss, were brought to England by Marquis of Wellesley and given to Mrs. St. John. Lamb was known as being a longhaired dog from Peking. The following Pugs have Lamb in their pedigrees: Tum Tum II; Comedy; Little Count; Dutchess of Connaught; Countess; Dowager; Zulu II, who was brought to America and known as Ch. Joe; Max; Bessie; and Kash. Moss was later owned by Lord Willoughby.

1871

· The Kennel Club of England was formed.

1875

· Click, the son of Lamb and Moss, was born and was a major contributor to the good show dogs in England and America. He was owned by Mrs. Laura Mayhew.

1876

· Punch, sired by Lord Willoughby's Jumbo, was a winner in England for the next two years. Punch was owned by Mr. T. Morris.

1878

· Ch. George was born and owned by Mrs. E. A. Pue of Philadelphia. He was described by Dr. Cryer in *The Prize Pugs of America and England* "as always being kept in fine condition and was never afraid in the ring. His color, condition, body, legs, feet, tail, nails, and symmetry were very good; on head mask, wrinkles, trace, coat, and neck he was fair. His ears were not good in shape nor well carried, and he was oversized, nearly twenty-five pounds." Ch. George was shown in Pittsburgh in 1882, where he earned first in open class and won the prize. He was also the first Pug registered by the American Kennel Club (AKC.)

· Bred by Mr. Thomas Morris of Bolton, England and owned by Dr. Cryer, Ch. Roderick was born on July 12, 1878. His sire was Punch and his dam was Judy. Roderick was a small dog, weighing about 14 and one-half pounds. He was very good in symmetry, size, body, feet, head, ears, mask, color, and coat. The forelegs were good, but hind legs were very weak.

1879

· Bred by M. Jameson of England and owned by Mr. George H. Hill of Madeira, Ohio, Ch. Joe was born on March 31, 1879 and was considered one of the best Pugs in America at the time. Ch. Joe was known as Zulu II in England.

• Owned and exhibited by Mrs. W. Fisher of Germantown, Pennsylvania, Punko was born in 1877. During a show in 1879, Punko became a winner by a misunderstanding. Dr. Cryer quoted, "Philadelphia Kennel Club had five entries in that year, and three judges made a display of their knowledge of Pugs by sending Roderick (sired by Lord Willoughby's Jumbo) out of the ring, disqualifying him for 'carrying his tail on the wrong side.' The first prize was given to Punko, a very indifferent specimen of the Pug. Punko was never shown again. The three wise men who gave him first prize did so probably because the Hon. John Welsh had bought him in London. Of course, the United States Minister at the Court of St. James would not send anything but a standard Pug to this country, and as Punko carried his tail on the left, which the judges considered the "right" side, he was awarded the first prize."

1880
• Lady Brassey returned from her voyage to China with black Pugs. At this time, the recognized color was fawn in its various shades, with traces of black.

1881
• Harriet Beecher Stowe, the author of *Uncle Tom's Cabin*, had two Pugs named Punch and Missy. Punch was stolen from Mrs. Stowe in 1883 and recovered at the New Haven Dog Show in March of 1885.
• First-year champion prizes were offered to Pugs in America.

1883
• The Pug Dog Club was formed in England by Mr. T. Proctor on January 26. The first secretary was Miss M. A. Holdsworth.

1884
• Ch. Bo-Peep was the first American-bred Pug to win a championship. She died in a fire on January 12, 1888, at the age of six. Bo-Peep was bred by A.W. Lucy of New York and owned by Mr. H. L. Goodman of Auburn, Illinois.

1885
• The American Kennel Club recognized the Pug breed.

1886
• The first black Pug named Jack Spratt was shown at the Maidenstone Show by Lady Brassey.

It is recorded that in 1790, the Pug's ears were either cropped or completely cut off to give him a more pleasing expression.

1891
· Charles van den Eycken created an oil painting titled *Willpower* that features a collared Pug and a friend gazing at a cake.
1896
· The *Ladies Kennel Journal* states that Queen Victoria had a black Pug that was an import from China.
1897
· The English Kennel Club opened separate color classes—black and fawn. Until 1880, fawn was the only recognized color for Pugs.

Caring for Your Pug

Feeding and Nutrition

The best way to make sure that your Pug puppy is receiving the correct amount and type of food for his age is to follow the diet sheet provided by the breeder from whom you obtained your puppy. Do your best not to change the puppy's diet in order to avoid digestive problems and diarrhea, which is serious in young puppies. Puppies with diarrhea can dehydrate very rapidly, causing severe problems and even death. If it is necessary to change your Pug puppy's diet for any reason, it should be done gradually. Begin by adding a few tablespoons of the new food and increasing the amount until the meal consists entirely of the new product.

At about six months of age, the Pug puppy can do well on three meals a day—morning, noon, and night. By the time your Pug is 10 to 12 months old, you can reduce feedings to 1 or 2 a day. The main meal can be given either in the morning or in the evening; it is really a matter of choice on your part. There are two important

The amount of food a dog is fed depends on his age. For example, 3 meals a day is sufficient for a 6-month-old Pug; 1 or 2 meals a day is sufficient for a 10- to 12-month-old Pug.

things to remember: Feed your Pug his main meal the same time every day and make sure that what you feed him is nutritionally complete.

The single meal can be supplemented by a morning or nighttime snack of hard dog biscuits made especially for small dogs. These biscuits are helpful in maintaining healthy gums and teeth and are yummy treats for your Pug.

Balanced Diets

In order for a canine diet to qualify as "complete and balanced" in the United States, it must meet standards set by the Subcommittee on Canine Nutrition of the National Research Council of the National Academy of Sciences. Most commercial dog foods meet these standards. The ingredients contained in the food are listed in descending order with the main ingredient listed first.

Refined sugars fed with any regularity at all can quickly cause your Pug to become obese and will definitely create tooth decay. Canine teeth are not genetically disposed to handling sugars, so it's best to avoid products that contain a high degree of sugar.

To maintain good health, a Pug needs fresh water on a daily basis and a properly prepared, balanced diet that contains the essential nutrients. Dog foods are available in many varieties: canned, dry, semi-moist, scientifically fortified, and all natural. Most supermarkets and pet stores carry a wide enough variety from which to choose.

All dogs, whether small or giant, are carnivorous (meat-eating) animals. The foundation of their diets should be made up of protein, which can be canned or dried. Check to make sure that the major ingredient (appearing first on the list) is in fact, animal protein.

Wild carnivores eat the entire beast that they capture and kill. The carnivore's prey consists almost entirely of herbivores (plant-eating animals). Invariably, the carnivore begins its meal with the contents of the herbivore's stomach, which provide the carbohydrates, minerals, and nutrients present in vegetables.

Through centuries of domestication, we have made our dogs entirely dependent on us for their well-being. Therefore, we are responsible for duplicating the food balance that the wild dog finds in nature. The domesticated dog's diet must include some protein, carbohydrates, fats, roughage, and small amounts of essential minerals and vitamins.

Feed your Pug a well-balanced, nutritious diet that includes the necessary amounts of proteins, carbohydrates, fats, minerals, and vitamins.

Finding commercially prepared diets that contain all the necessary nutrients in the proper balance will not present a problem. However, it is important to understand that these commercially prepared foods do contain most of the nutrients your Pug requires. Most Pug breeders recommend vitamin supplementation for healthy coats and increased stamina, especially for show dogs, pregnant bitches, and growing puppies.

Homemade dog food is a growing trend among breeders today. By combining their special mixture of vegetables and animal protein, breeders eliminate the preservatives that are found in many commercially prepared foods from their dogs' diets. It is important to discuss this feeding method with your veterinarian so that you are sure to include all the necessary nutrients your dog requires.

Table scraps should be given only as part of the dog's meal and never from the table. A Pug that becomes accustomed to being hand-fed from the table can quickly become a real pest at mealtime. Also, dinner guests may find the pleading stare and vocalization of your Pug less than appealing when dinner is being served.

Dogs do not care if food looks like a hot dog or a piece of cheese. Truly nutritious dog foods are seldom manufactured to look like food that appeals to humans. Dogs only care about how food smells and tastes. It is highly doubtful you will be eating your dog's food, so do not waste your money on these look-alike products.

Oversupplementation

A great deal of controversy exists today regarding the orthopedic problems that afflict many breeds. Some claim these problems are entirely hereditary conditions, but many others feel that they can be exacerbated by overuse of mineral and vitamin supplements for puppies. Oversupplementation is now regarded by some breeders as a major contributor to many skeletal abnormalities found in today's purebred dogs. When giving vitamin supplementation, one should *never* exceed the prescribed amount. No vitamin, however, is a substitute for a nutritious, balanced diet. Although pregnant and lactating bitches do require supplementation of some kind, do not exceed the prescribed dose. Extreme caution is advised in this case and best discussed with your veterinarian.

Special Diets

There are now a number of commercially prepared diets for dogs with special dietary needs. The overweight, underweight, or geriatric dog can have his nutritional needs met by adjusting the calorie content of these foods accordingly. With the right foods and the proper amount of exercise, your Pug should stay in top shape. Again, common sense must prevail. Too many calories will increase weight; too few calories will reduce weight.

Occasionally, a young Pug that is teething will become a poor eater. The concerned owner's first response is to tempt the dog by hand-feeding him special treats and foods, which the problem eater seems to prefer. However, this practice only serves to compound the problem. Once the dog learns to play the waiting game, he will turn up his nose at anything other than his favorite food, knowing

You can determine the effectiveness of your Pug's diet by looking at his appearance. He should be well covered with flesh and show good bone and muscle development.

full well that what he wants to eat will eventually arrive.

Unlike humans, dogs have no suicidal tendencies. A healthy dog will not starve himself to death. He may not eat enough to stay in perfect physical condition, but he will definitely eat enough to maintain himself. If your Pug is not eating properly and appears to be too thin, it is probably best to consult your veterinarian. However, the opposite condition will more likely be the case. Pugs have notoriously healthy appetites.

Carefully monitoring your Pug's weight will help increase the longevity of his life and maintain good health.

Pugs are usually not fussy eaters; most are ready, willing, and able to consume their morning and evening meals long before it is time for you to serve them. In fact, Pugs would be happy if they were given a constant supply of snacks throughout the day. We're not accusing Pugs of being gluttons, but it must be said that they will take just about any meal you give them with little regard to their waistlines. However, do not be persuaded into overfeeding your Pug.

A Pug's health and longevity depend on how well he maintains a reasonable weight for his size. Excessive weight can create a myriad of skeletal problems for a Pug, not to mention the deleterious effect it has on the dog's heart.

It is impossible to give an appropriate ideal weight for all Pugs; amount of bone and age contribute heavily to the variables. Your Pug is most likely the proper weight if you are able to feel his backbone and ribs through a moderate padding of flesh.

THE PUG'S SPECIAL NEEDS

Heat and Your Pug

The short-nosed (brachycephalic) construction of the Pug requires very special care in hot weather. Anyone who wants a

Pug must clearly understand these needs and be willing to accept the responsibility for ensuring their dog's health.

Owners should adhere to the hot weather rule, which is no playing, particularly in the sun, when temperatures and humidity are high. Many Pug owners consider any temperature above 80 degrees as "hot weather time" and should initiate necessary precautions.

If your Pug is overheated and becomes extremely distressed, wrap him in cold towels and get him to a veterinarian at once. The best way to avoid heat-induced trauma is to be constantly aware of the temperature and not to allow your Pug to become involved in any stressful situations.

Travel

It's a rule that owners must never leave their dogs in a situation where they are exposed to direct sunlight. Although heat problems encountered while traveling can be minimized with air-conditioned cars, never leave your dog in an unconditioned car in hot weather. Once you arrive at your destination, get your Pug into a cool shaded area immediately. If you are forced to keep your Pug in the sun for a brief period, put a wet towel over his body and head and remember to keep him off asphalt or concrete.

If there is no air-conditioning at your destination and the weather is extremely hot, gradually decrease the air-conditioning in your car so that you will not have to take your Pug from a cold vehicle into high heat. This is too much of a shock and can cause serious problems. Needless to say, you must never leave your Pug alone in an automobile. Even on

The Pug's brachycephalic construction makes him sensitive to the hot weather. Keep your Pug indoors when the temperatures are too high.

overcast days, temperatures can soar in just minutes. Small battery-operated fans are a great way of keeping your Pug cool and could be instrumental in avoiding serious complications.

Although you may want to take your Pug along on your summer vacation, consider the situation carefully. It will take a great deal of planning and will restrict your freedom considerably. Your Pug is much better off staying at home where he can be carefully supervised. If you absolutely have to leave your dog at a boarding kennel, do not leave him in a place that has not had documented experience in taking care of Pugs. Your breeder or veterinarian may be able to recommend a reputable kennel.

If air travel is on your Pug's schedule, discuss this matter with your veterinarian. He or she might advise tranquilizing your dog to preclude stress. Oxygen deprivation during flights is a serious threat to your Pug. Further, most baggage attendants have no idea how dangerous it is to allow your Pug's shipping container to sit on the tarmac in the hot sun. No matter how many dogs you may have owned in the past, when it comes to Pugs and heat, the situation is entirely different!

Exercise

Proper exercise is vital to your Pug's health. Because of the Pug's intolerance for the heat, be sure to conduct all physical

In addition to feeding and grooming, exercise should be a part of your Pug's daily routine. However, it's best to conduct any physical activity in cool weather.

activities in the cool weather hours, such as early morning or evening. If your own exercise proclivities are closer to a leisurely walk around the block than to a strenuous ten-mile run, choosing a Pug was a wise decision. The Pug is not a breed that requires you to take your energy level to its outer limits. If there are children or another dog in your home, then your Pug may be getting all the exercise he needs to stay fit. However, this does not mean that your Pug will not benefit from a daily walk around the park. On the contrary, steady exercise that keeps your canine companion's heart rate in the low working area will extend his life. In addition to spending quality time together, exercising with your Pug increases the chances that the both of you will enjoy each other's company for many years to come.

If you exercise your Pug at the proper time and gradually increase the level, there is absolutely no reason why you and your Pug should not be able to work up to a daily mile walk at a reasonable pace.

Toys and Chewing

Pugs, even as puppies, have great jaw strength for their small size, and although they are not notorious chewers, some can be very destructive during their teething period. It is said that a Pug puppy is part private investigator and part vacuum cleaner; they find things that have yet to be lost and feel everything they find should be filed in their tummies.

Puppy-proofing your home is a must. Your curious Pug will have a knack for getting into things he shouldn't, so you have to outsmart him and prevent him from wandering into possible danger.

Provide your Pug with safe toys that will keep him busy and eliminate his need for eating your needlepoint pillow or the upholstery on your favorite chair. Be sure to give him toys that are hard to chew up and not gummy or soft. Pugs also love all types of shoes. Dogs are unable to differentiate between your dirty old sneakers and your brand new expensive loafers, so never leave your shoes hanging around the house.

Socialization

By nature, the Pug is a happy dog and takes most situations in stride. However, it is important to accommodate the breed's natural instincts by making sure your dog is accustomed to

Providing your Pug with safe, durable chew toys, like an old shoe, will keep him occupied and prevent him from chewing the furniture.

various everyday events. Traffic, strange noises, loud or hyperactive children, and unfamiliar animals can be very intimidating to a dog of any breed that has never experienced them before. Gently and gradually introduce your puppy to as many new situations as you possibly can. Make it a habit to take your Pug along whenever it's possible. The Pug is a real crowd-pleaser, and you will find that your dog will savor all the attention he gets.

GROOMING YOUR PUG

Although the Pug does not have a long coat to contend with, grooming is still a requirement. Regular grooming not only improves your Pug's health and appearance, it eliminates any doggy odor that he might develop.

Your puppy should become accustomed to standing quietly on a grooming table for his weekly once-over. A stiff bristle brush will whisk away what little debris your Pug's coat holds, and a soft towel will restore the coat's shine.

Always brush the hair in the same direction that it grows, beginning at the dog's head, then brushing toward the tail and down the sides and legs. This procedure will loosen the dead hair and brush it off the dog. This is also a good time to check the skin thoroughly for any abrasions or external parasites.

Removing the face whiskers is optional. Some owners feel that the long whiskers detract from the Pug's natural expression. If you decide to remove the whiskers, do so with a pair of blunt-edged curved scissors. Never attempt to use straight-edged pointed scissors around a Pug's face. The Pug's eyes are prominent and a sudden movement on the dog's part could cause him serious injury. A quick reminder: Never allow your Pug to hang his head out of the window of your moving car. Flying debris can cause serious damage to his eyes.

While your Pug is on the grooming table, check the skin inside his thighs and armpits to see if it is dry or red. Artificial heat during winter months can dry out the skin and cause it to become chapped. If this is the case, rub a small amount of petroleum jelly or baby oil over the dry areas.

Some Pugs are subject to dry noses. In extreme cases, the nose leather can shrivel and crack. Avoid this by regularly applying petroleum jelly to the nose.

Nail Trimming

Pugs seldom get enough exercise on rough surfaces, which helps wear their nails down. Clip or file your Pug's nails on a regular basis. A Pug uses his feet like we use our hands and long nails can injure his eyes, so keep his nails trimmed short. Grooming time is also a good time to accustom your dog to having his feet inspected for cracked pads. Pay particular attention to any swollen or tender areas and be sure to check between the toes for splinters and thorns.

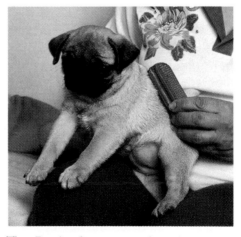

The Pug's short coat doesn't require much grooming; however, a weekly brushing will improve his health and appearance and will eliminate any foul odor he may develop.

Foxtail is a weed that grows in many parts of the country. Its seedpod is released in small barb with a hook on its end

Trimming your Pug's nails is an important part of his grooming routine. Also check for cracked footpads and tender or swollen areas.

and can easily find its way into a Pug's foot or between his toes. This barb will very quickly work its way deep into the dog's flesh causing soreness and infection and should be removed by your veterinarian before serious problems result.

The Pug's nails can grow long very rapidly. Do not allow the nails to become overgrown and then expect to cut them back easily. Each nail has a blood vessel running through the center called the quick, which grows close to the end of the nail and contains very sensitive nerve endings. If the nail isn't trimmed, it will be impossible to cut it back to a proper length without cutting into the quick. This causes the dog severe pain and can result in a great deal of bleeding, which can be very difficult to stop.

Nails can be trimmed with canine nail clippers, an electric nail grinder (also called a drummel), or a coarse file made specifically for trimming. All three of these items can be purchased at major pet emporiums.

We prefer the electric nail grinder because it is so easy to control and helps avoid cutting into the quick. Dark nails make it practically impossible to see where the quick ends. Regardless of which nail-trimming device is used, one must proceed with caution and remove only a small portion of the nail at a time.

If you choose to use the electric grinder, introduce it to your puppy at an early age. The instrument has a whining sound not unlike that of a dentist's drill, which, combined with the vibration of the sanding head on the nail itself, can take some getting used to. However, most dogs we have used it on eventually accept it as one of life's trials.

If the quick gets nipped in the trimming process, there are a number of blood clotting products available at pet shops that will almost immediately stem the flow of blood. It is wise to have one of these products on hand in case there is a nail trimming accident or if the dog tears a nail on his own.

Bathing

If you brush your Pug on a regular basis, bathing will seldom be necessary, unless he finds his way into something that leaves his coat with a disagreeable odor. Even then, there are many products available, both dry and liquid, that eliminate odors and leave the coat shiny and clean without having to resort to a wet bath.

If your Pug has given himself a mud bath, cleaning him with a damp wash cloth will suffice. However, if your Pug's coat becomes wet in the cold weather, be sure to towel dry him thoroughly. The Pug is a thin-coated breed and has no undercoat to protect him from a draft or winter chill!

When a wet bath is necessary, use a shampoo made especially for dogs, and place cotton in the ear canals to prevent water from entering this delicate area. Soak the dog with a shower hose and be careful not to let water run into your Pug's nose.

Lather the coat twice, thoroughly rinsing each time to make sure that all shampoo residue is removed, which can cause dry skin and irritation if left in the coat.

A drop of mineral oil or a tiny dab of petroleum jelly in each eye will protect the Pug's eyes from any shampoo sting. Even if you use a non-irritating shampoo, it's still a good idea to use a lubricant.

Although this bubble bath looks like fun, Pugs seldom need baths. However, if your Pug has been playing in the mud, you will need to clean his coat with a damp washcloth.

THE STANDARD for the Pug

THE BREEDERS' CRITERION

The standard is a guideline that helps to provide a mental picture of the perfect Pug. This instrument is not a precise blueprint, but leaves areas to be subjectively interpreted. Many Pugs have all the parts, but the parts are not in balance. This tool should be used as a guide to improve the Pug.

Although the standard does not mention soundness, it cannot be overlooked. For years, the Pug Dog Club of America has been working on an illustrated standard to help clarify the written standard. The illustrated standard is an excellent tool to assist breeders, Pug lovers, and judges. Experience, research, and communicating with respected breeders are the best ways to help one understand the standard. Each of the written standards is helpful and can enhance your ideal blueprint of what is the perfect Pug.

THE STONEHENGE PUG STANDARD

The first Pug standard was written by Stonehenge and published in *The Dogs of the British Isles.* The English were the first to revise the Stonehenge standard with the use of Hugh Dalziel's work, and later, the Americans copied and adjusted the English standard. The Pug standard becomes slightly more explicit each time it's retailored. When modifying a standard, many issues develop that cause difficulties among breeders. Many breeders will not agree with a particular point or will feel that a component is not being developed or an item has little importance, such as the facial mole. The facial mole with three hairs that is mentioned in the Stonehenge standard has been part of every existing Pug and still exists today. When Hugh Dalziel revised the Stonehenge book, he felt that the Pug's facial mole had little importance and so it was deleted from the standard. The facial mole is one item that we have not been consciously breeding for, but it has continued to be part of our Pugs through multiple generations. The trace, on the other hand, has been mentioned in the Stonehenge book and in every other standard, even the revised AKC standard, but today it exists only on a few Pugs. In the show ring, many prefer the lightest color coat that sometimes lacks pigmentation on the muzzle, the ears, the nails, and the trace. Most Pugs are born with

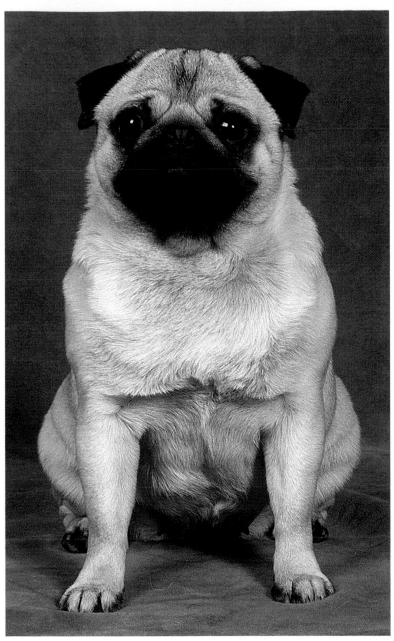

The breed standard explains what the ideal Pug should look and act like.

Only fawn-colored Pugs are accepted in the Stonehenge standard.

a trace but it appears to fade as they mature. Today, the dark trace is a highlight that is a shade darker than the coat and should be a thin line that goes from the back of the neck to the tail. If the breeders wished to darken the trace on the Pug and desired it to be an issue, they still could darken it with selective breeding. The Stonehenge standard includes a point chart that enables a breeder to decide what is the most important part of the Pug. The trace is only worth 5 points out of 100 points total, therefore it is not of great importance to many breeders.

In the Stonehenge standard, the English standard, and the original American standard there are point charts that give an allotment of points for each item. When the AKC had the parent club standardize the standard, the point chart was eliminated, but in the illustrated standard, the parent club has included a point chart. The Stonehenge standard gives a total of 40 points for the body, 35 points for the head, and 25 points for coat and color. This standard gave the body the most points, telling breeders that the body or the structure is the most important area, followed by the head. The Stonehenge is the only standard that mentions other dog breeds for comparisons and crossbreeding with the Bulldog.

The Stonehenge standard is a great reference for the breed. It makes the comparison of the two strands of Pugs in England and accepts both types—the Willoughby and the Morrison. Black Pugs are not included in this standard, only fawns. The section on color has great value, stating that the Morrison Pug is a rich fawn, pure and unmixed with any darker shades. The salmon fawn, which was later called apricot fawn, is not preferred and the specimens carrying this color are of poor quality. The Willoughby Pug is cold stone or a drab color of fawn tipped with black hair, possibly the color smutt and/or the color silver. At the turn of the century, Mr. Reginald Mayhew stated that Willoughby was a prominent factor in Pugdom and Willoughby's Pugs were popular and a common name. Mr. Mayhew recalled that he saw so many Pugs born practically black and consigned to the bucket that the introduction of the black was a novelty.

Another item of interest is the lolling tongue, which is considered a fault today and is not accepted, as it was in the late 1800s. The Stonehenge standard states that a Pug should be 10 to 12 inches tall and does not quote a weight. Mr. Stonehenge's statement on size gives a better description for size than any other standard. Many past and present breeders have argued over the size of the Pugs. A height of 12 inches tells you that the Pug will also be approximately 12 inches long, due to the Pug being symmetrically balanced. Weight can vary so much from one Pug to another depending on the amount of bone and the hardness of muscles that height is possibly the best indicator of size.

Point Count for the Stonehenge Standard

Head	10
Ears	5
Eyes	5
Moles	5
Mask, Vent, and Wrinkles	10
Trace	5
Color	10
Coat	10
Neck	5
Body	10
Legs and Feet	10
Tail	10
Symmetry and Size	5
Total Points	100

The **head** should have a round monkey-like skull and should be of considerable girth, but in proportion and not so great as that of the Bulldog's.

According to the Stonehenge standard, the Pug's head should have a round monkey-like skull and should be of considerable girth.

The **face** is short, but again, not bully or retreating, the end being cut off square and the teeth must be level. If undershot, a cross of the bull is almost always to be relied on. The tongue is large and often hanging out of the mouth. The cheek is very full and muscular.

The **ears** are small, vine-shaped, and thin, and should be moderately flat on the face; formerly they were invariably closely cropped, but this practice is now quite out of fashion. They are black with a slight mixture of fawn hair.

The **eyes** are brown and full with a soft expression. There should be no tendency to weep, as in the Toy spaniel.

A **black mole** is always demanded on each cheek, with two or three hairs springing from it; the regulation number of these is three, but of course, it is easy to reduce them to that number.

Mask, vent, and wrinkles must be taken together, as they all depend mainly on color. The wrinkles, it is true, are partly in the skin, but over and above these there should be lines of black corresponding with them on the face and forehead. The mask should extend over the whole face as jet black, reaching over the eyes, and the vent also should be of the same color. In the Willoughby strain, the black generally extends higher up the skull, and does not have the same definite edge as in the Morrison Pug, in which this point is well shown and greatly insisted on by his admirers.

A **trace,** or black line, is exhibited along the top of the back by all perfect Pugs, and the clearer this is the better. The definition is clearer in the Morrison than in the Willoughby Pug. When it extends widely over the back it is called a "saddle mark," and this is often displayed in the Willoughby, though seldom met with in the Morrison strain.

The **color** of the Morrison Pug is a rich fawn, while that of the Willoughby is a cold stone. The salmon fawn is never met with in good specimens of either and is objectable. In the Willoughby, the fawn-colored hairs are apt to be tipped with black, but in its rival, the fawn color is pure and unmixed with any darker shade. Of course, in interbred specimens, the color is often intermediate.

The **coat** is short, soft, and glossy over the whole body, but on the tail, it is longer and rougher. A fine tail indicates a bull cross.

The **neck** is full, stout and muscular, but without any tendency to dewlap.

The **body** is very thick and strong, with a wide crest and round ribs. The loins should be very muscular, as well as the quarters, giving a general punchy look, almost peculiar to this dog.

The **legs** should be straight but fine in bone, and well clothed with muscle. As for the feet, they must be small, and in any case, narrow. In both strains, the toes are well split-up, but in the Willoughby, the shape of the foot is cat-like, while the Morrison strain has a hare foot. There should be no white on the toes and the nails should be dark.

The **tail** must curve so that it lies flat on the side, not rising above the back to such an extent as to show daylight through it. The curl should extend to a little more than one circle.

The Pug's wide-eyed, gentle expression is one of his most endearing characteristics.

Although the ideal Pug is small—only 10 to 12 inches high—his body is very thick and strong.

In **size**, the Pug should be from 10 to 12 inches high—the smaller the better. A good specimen should be very symmetrical.

THE ORIGINAL ENGLISH PUG CLUB STANDARD

This original English Pug Club standard was accepted in 1887 and is the basis for the American standard. The English standard emphasized that the Pug should be symmetrical with balance and used the expression *multum in parvo*, meaning a lot in a small package. This standard does not make a comparison of different lines or mention other breeds for reference. The English were concerned about size, balance, and wrinkles. They gave 40 points for the body, emphasizing a symmetrical body, 25 points for color and coat, and 35 points on the head, emphasizing the eyes being round, dark, and full of fire. This standard has two colors, and still the black was not included until 1897. The English standard was based on Hugh Dalziel's *The British Dogs,* and the information obtained from the Stonehenge Pug standard.

Symmetry 10
Size 5
Condition 5
Body 10
Legs 5
Feet 5
Head 5
Muzzle 5
Ears 5
Eyes 10
Mask 5
Wrinkles 5
Tail 5
Trace 5
Coat 5
Color 5
General Carriage 5
Total Points 100

Symmetry–Symmetry and general appearance, decidedly square and cobby. A lean, leggy Pug and a dog with short legs and long body are equally objectionable.

Size and Condition–The Pug should be *multum in parvo*, but this condensation should be shown by compactness of form, well-knit proportions, and hardness of developed muscles. Weight to be from 13 to 17 pounds (dog or bitch).

Body–Short and cobby, wide in chest, and well ribbed-up.

Legs–Very strong, straight, of moderate length, and set well under.

Feet–Neither so long as the foot of the hare nor so round as that of the cat, well split-up toes, and black nails.

Muzzle–Short, blunt, square, but not up-faced.

Head–Large, massive, round–not apple-headed–with no indentation of the skull.

Eyes–Dark in color, very large, bold, and prominent, globular in shape, soft and solicitous in expression, very lustrous, and when excited, full of fire.

Ears–Thin, small, and soft, like black velvet. There are two kinds: the rose and the button. Preference is given to the latter.

Markings–Clearly defined. The muzzle or mask, ears, moles on cheek, thumb marks, or diamond on forehead, back trace should be as black as possible.

In 1947, a revision to the Pug's weight was made in the English Pug Club standard. The weight standard was raised to 14 to 18 pounds, which is the current weight.

Mask–The mask should be black; the more intense and defined, the better.

Wrinkles–Large and deep.

Trace–A black line extending from the occiput to the tail.

Tail–Curled tightly over the hip. The double curl is perfection.

Coat–Fine, smooth, soft, neither hard nor woolly.

Color–Silver or apricot fawn. Each should be decided to make the contrast complete between the color and the trace and mask.

AMERICA ACCEPTS THE ENGLISH STANDARD

In 1946 or 1947, the Original English Pug Club standard was revised and the only alteration made was in weight, which is now 14-18 pounds. In the United States, the first standard was published in 1929, according to Roy Carlberg, Secretary of the American Kennel Club. In 1967, Mr. Carlberg stated that the American standard was "printed by courtesy of the Pug Dog Club of England." In 1963, many breeders wanted to add comments to the standard to make it clearer. A committee was formed and headed by Louise Gore, a prominent respected pioneer of the breed, and their suggestions were reviewed.

The breeders in 1967 suggested keeping the original English standard that the AKC had accepted and add the following after each section, but the suggestions were never accepted by the Pug Dog Club of America. The committee's comments are included to help the reader create a better picture. All standards are subjectively interpreted, but if the descriptions are clear and precise, then the subjective opinions will be more in constant agreement.

The AKC Standard with Breeders' Comments of 1967

Symmetry—Symmetry and general appearance, decidedly square and cobby. A lean, leggy Pug and dog with short legs and a long body are equally objectionable.

* A boxy, balanced appearance—a dog of heavy bone compactly put together. Tuck-up not desirable.

Size and Condition—The Pug should be *multum in parvo,* but this condensation (if the word may be used) should be shown in compactness of form, well-knit proportions, and hardness of developed muscle. Weight from 14 to 18 pounds (dog or bitch) desirable.

* No one feature of the Pug should be so prominent as to cause him to appear out of proportion. Preference should be given to the Pug nearest the desired weight, when the quality is equal.

Body—Short and cobby, wide in chest. Pug should be wide, both front and rear to ensure desired cobbiness, and well ribbed up.

* The back should be neither roached nor swayed.

Legs—Very strong, straight, of moderate length, and well under.

* Well-muscled to give balanced support. Pasterns well-up from the toes, thus ensuring a firm gait, neither plodding or paddling.

Feet—Neither so long as the foot of the hare, nor so round as that of the cat, well split-up toes, and black nails.

* Toes that turn neither in nor out are desirable.

Muzzle—Short, blunt, square, but not up-faced.

* Nose should be short, black, and wide. Jaws broad and square. The bite should be very slightly undershot or even to ensure squareness. Chops should completely cover the teeth and tongue without lippiness.

Head—Large, massive, round (not apple-headed), with no indentation of the skull.

* Round means both from front view and in profile. Size of head to be determined by the size of the complete Pug. Nothing should detract from the symmetry. Head should be carried gracefully on a short neck, slightly arched.

Eyes—Dark in color, very large, bold and prominent, globular in shape, soft and solicitous in expression, very lustrous, and when excited, full of fire.

* Set well apart and looking forward.

Ears—Thin, small, soft, like black velvet. There are two kinds: the rose and the button. Preference is given to the latter.

Markings—Clearly defined. The muzzle or mask, ears, moles on cheeks, thumb mark or diamond on forehead, back trace should be as black as possible.

Mask—The mask should be black. The more intense and well defined it is, the better.

Wrinkles—Large and deep.

* They should be clearly defined. The large over-nose roll wrinkle is desirable to enhance the roundness of the head.

Trace—A black line extending from the occiput to the tail.

Tail—Curled tightly as possible over the hip. The double curl is perfection.

* The tail set high on the rump is desirable to give squareness to the Pug. A tucked or drooping tail should be penalized as this fault spoils the symmetry of the Pug.

Coat—Fine, smooth, short, and glossy, neither hard nor woolly.

Color—Silver, apricot fawn, or black. Each should be decided to make the contrast complete between the color, the trace, and the mask.

The breeders at this time felt that the Pug was to be symmetrical and in balance. They were concerned with details in the head and placement, color, and direction of the eyes. The wrinkles should be clearly defined along with the other head markings and the muzzle black and square with proper teeth to fill the lower broad jaw, with short lips and little black ears. Again, they state nothing should detract from symmetry. The size of the head is to be in balance with the entire body. The breeders wanted an appealing head in which the features are properly placed and clearly defined. The body that is balanced and square completed the package. During this time and today, many judges look for a large size head and do not look for a balanced head with correct facial features. The head in a balanced Pug will not be excessive in size.

STANDARDIZATION OF THE PUG DOG CLUB OF AMERICA STANDARD

The American Kennel Club asked the Pug Dog Club of America to revise or add lacking information to the Pug standard. The AKC wanted to have the standards of all breeds in a uniform style, in order to make learning easier for judges and breeders. Revising the standard caused aggravation for many. Some breeders wanted changing or updating. Others were concerned that breeders who were working on the committee would encourage their own Pug's style. The majority felt that the Pug standard had stood for 100 years and the Pug had steadily improved and was a healthy breed. With an "if it's not broken don't try to fix it" attitude, along with the strong sense of keeping tradition, the membership decided to keep the existing standard in its complete form and only add information that the American Kennel Club requested. By keeping the standard intact, the issue of weight would not be open for discussion and this alone saved many breeders' friendships.

The items that the AKC requested that the Pug Dog Club of America add to their 100-year-old standard to complete the standardization of the standard were the following:

Bite—A Pug's bite should be very slightly undershot.

* Note that "very slightly" is a subjective term; what is slightly undershot to me might not be the same amount to another breeder.

Topline—The short body is level from the withers to the high-set tail.

Hindquarters—The strong, powerful hindquarters have moderate bend of stifle and short hocks perpendicular to the ground. The legs are parallel when viewed from behind. The hindquarters are in balance with the forequarters. The thighs and buttocks are full and muscular.

Gait—Viewed from the front, the forelegs should be carried well forward, showing no weakness in the pasterns, the paws landing squarely with the central toes straight ahead. The rear action should

The ideal Pug should exhibit playfulness, charm, and an extroverted, loving disposition.

be strong and free through the hocks and stifles, with no twisting or turning in or out at front. The hind legs should follow in line with the front. There is a slight natural convergence of the limbs both fore and aft as speed increases. A slight roll of the hindquarters typifies the gait, which should be free, self-assured, and jaunty.

Temperament—This is an even-tempered breed that exhibits stability, playfulness, great charm, dignity, and an outgoing, loving disposition.

Neck—The neck is slightly arched. It is strong, thick, and with enough length to carry the head proudly.

THE ILLUSTRATED STANDARD

The illustrated standard is a good tool for breeders, judges, exhibitors, and Pug owners to aid in forming a correct image of a perfect Pug. All of the members of the committees that worked on this standard have put great effort in trying to emphasize the positive qualities of the Pug. The AKC, with the help of the Illustrated Standard Committee, created the computer-generated pictures for the illustrated standard.

General Appearance—Symmetry and general appearance are decidedly square and cobby. A lean, leggy Pug and a dog with short legs and a long body are equally objectionable.

Clarification:

The Pug should give a strong impression of squareness when viewed form any angle. Cobby means short bodied, thick set, and square. All of the parts must fit together to form a harmonious unit. The most important concept to remember is square.

Undesirable—A lean, leggy, terrier-type or a Pug with short legs and a long body.

Size, Proportion, Substance—The Pug should be *multum in parvo,* and this condensation (if the word may be used) is shown by compactness of form, well-knit proportions, and hardness of developed muscle. Weight from 14 to 18 pounds (dogs or bitches) desirable.

Proportion—Square.

Clarification:

The standard describes size only in terms of weight. The Pug's weight has to be in proportion to his height and bone. However, weight varies considerably according to body structure and density so that two Pugs of exactly the same measurements can

According to the standard, the Pug should be symmetrical and square-bodied.

vary as much as three pounds. The Pug should be evaluated on his bone, muscle, and cobbiness in relation to his size and estimated weight. Keep in mind that the Pug is a Toy breed.

Undesirable—Excessively large or diminutive. Lacking in muscle tone.

Head—The head is large, massive, round—not apple-headed—with no indentation of the skull.

Clarification:

The head should be broad and round when viewed from front and flat when viewed from the side, neither up-faced (too much chin) or down-faced (not enough chin). A large head is essential, but a head so large as to be out of balance with the rest of the dog is as unappealing as a small-headed Pug. The Pug's head must be in proportion with the whole dog.

Undesirable—Lack of balance, up-faced, protruding nose.

Nose—Although the standard does not mention the nose; a short discussion is necessary. The nose is black, wide (not pinched), and lies flat, bisecting the eyes. The stop is concealed by an over-nose wrinkle. An unbroken wrinkle over the bridge of the nose unifies the face. A skimpy or split nose roll on an otherwise splendid specimen is permissible.

Undersirable—Dudley or butterfly nose, pinched nostrils, split or lack of nose roll.

Eyes—The eyes are dark in color, very large, bold and prominent, globular in shape, soft and solicitous in expression, very lustrous, and when excited, full of fire.

Clarification:

The large, dark appealing eyes of the Pug are an important feature. Eyes should be large, bold, and globular, but not bulging. A Pug's expression is largely dependent on the eyes. At rest, the expression should be benign, intelligent, and affectionate; when alert, the expression should be keen, curious, and very sparkling, showing a love of mischief.

While the standard makes no mention of eye position, it is accepted that the eyes shall be set well apart. The center of the eyes shall be in line with the top of the nose. Rims are black and usually encompassed by the black mask in the fawn Pug. East-west eyes are sometimes found, especially in puppies. Expression, size, shape, and color of the eye are the primary considerations.

Undesirable—White around eyes, almond shaped, squinted, or bulging eyes, east-west, close-set, or high-set eyes.

Very Undesirable—Light colored or small eyes.

Ears—The ears are thin, small, soft, like black velvet. There are two kinds: the rose and the button. Preference is given to the latter.

Clarification:

The ears should be set wide on the head. The fold of the button ear is level with the top of the skull. The ear should not drop below the outside corner of the eye when alert. The rose ear in Pugs appears smaller and is folded with the inner edge against the side of the head so not to show the inner burr as in Bulldogs. Flying button ears are not rose ears. The rose ear is small and neat, and tends to give the head a smaller, more rounded look. The size and the shape of the ear should be in balance with the overall size and shape of the head. Ears must be black and both should be of the same type.

Undesirable—Flying ears, light-colored ears, ears set too low or too high, ears too thick or too large.

Wrinkles—The wrinkles are large and deep.

Clarification:

Important to the breed's typical expression are the head wrinkles. The wrinkles of the forehead should be deep and set off by a darkening within the fold of the wrinkles in fawns. Wrinkles can, however, conceal an incorrect skull shape. To judge the head properly, the lead should be dropped so the head is up naturally and the bone structure can be examined more easily. The surplus skin under the throat and around the face is, in the Pug, a breed characteristic. It should be present in a large fold with wrinkles forming a ruff.

Undesirable—Plain (unwrinkled) face, lack of loose skin.

Muzzle—The muzzle is short, blunt, square, but not up-faced.

Clarification:

The muzzle, being approximately one-half of the face, is extremely important. It should be as flat as possible when viewed in profile. The cushioning of the muzzle should appear to equal the width of the skull. The upper lips should be full but not long enough to hide the chin. The under jaw is wide and deep and creates a definite chin. The muzzle should not fall away under the eyes, distorting head balance into an elongated rectangle.

Very Undesirable—Up-faced, narrow, or pointed muzzle. Too much or lack of underjaw. Pendulous lips. Falling away under the eyes.

Bite—A Pug's bite should be very slightly undershot.

Clarification:

An overbite distorts expression and sometimes gives a lippy, weak look to the face. Too much underbite gives the face an uptilt. A lolling or peeking tongue is evidence of malocclusion (wry mouth) and should be penalized.

We suggest the bite examination be the last part of the table examination. It is easiest to check the bite of the Pug by gently lifting the lip to the center.

Very undesirable—A Pug with teeth showing, a wry mouth or a lolling/peeking tongue.

Neck—The neck is slightly arched. It is strong, thick, and with enough length to carry the head proudly.

Clarification:

The head and body should be joined by a strong, well-muscled neck with enough length to carry the head proudly. The neck should have a slight rise or crest behind the skull, and should increase in breadth as it blends smoothly into the shoulders. Where the shoulder blade lies in relation to the backbone determines the appearance of neck length. The skin on the neck should be loose but fit smoothly.

Undesirable—Thin neck, neck too long or too short, tight skin.

Topline, Body—The short back is level from the withers to the high-set tail. The body is short and cobby, wide in chest, and well ribbed-up.

Clarification:

The body should give the strong impression of thick-set squareness. The appearance of a short back is most desirable. Elbows should fit close to the body, and should turn neither in nor out while the Pug is standing or moving. The topline should be level from withers to the tail set, and the tail should be set high. The underline should continue the cobby appearance with no obvious tuck-up. A well ribbed-up Pug will have a broad chest with the sternum protruding forward of the front assembly. However, an abnormal projection of the breastbone (pigeon-breast) is undesirable. Moderate loose skin down the back is matter of personal preference. The structure under the skin is the primary concern.

Undesirable—Low at the shoulders, roached or sway backed, sloping croup, a narrow chest, excessive tuck-up, a lean, rangy body, slabsides, pigeon-breasted, too fat or too soft, skin either too tight or overdone.

Along with bold, expressive eyes, the curled tail is another distinctive Pug characteristic. A double-curled tail is considered perfection.

Tail–The tail is curled as tightly as possible over the hip. The double curl is perfection.

Clarification:

The tail is another very distinctive Pug characteristic. It must be set well up on the back. A double curl is perfect, but a tight single or one-and-a-half curl should not be faulted. While the standard states the tail shall be carried over the hip, it is now generally accepted that it may be carried on top of the back as well.

Undesirable–A floppy, loose curl not carried tight to the body, less than a single curl, low-set tail, tail too thin or carried uncurled.

Forequarters–The legs are very strong, straight, of moderate length, and are set well under. The elbows should be directly under the withers when viewed from the side. The shoulders are moderately laid back.

Clarification:

Very strong legs mean substantial in bone and hard muscle. Viewed from the front, legs must be straight down from the elbow. Some Pugs have a muscle build-up on the outside of the fore legs; this is permissible only if the inside line of the leg is straight. The Pug should never give the impression of a bowed front. Viewed from the side, elbow should be directly under the point of withers, thus setting the legs well under. The chest should be rounded out past the point of the shoulders.

The Pug's legs should be very strong, straight, and of moderate length.

Undesirable—Steep shoulders, short upper arm, fiddle front, loose elbows, legs too short or too long, lack of forechest.

Feet—The feet are neither so long as the foot of the hare, nor so round as that of the cat. Well split-up toes and the nails black. Dewclaws are generally removed.

Pasterns—The pasterns are strong, neither steep nor down.

Clarification:

A Pug's feet are more oval than round, with well-split-up toes and thick pads. The nails should be black, but if a light-nailed Pug is obviously better, he should not be overly penalized.

Undesirable—Straight or broken down pasterns, flat feet, splayed feet, white nails.

Hindquarters—The strong, powerful hindquarters have moderate bend of stifle and short hocks perpendicular to the ground. The legs are parallel when viewed from behind. The hindquarters are in balance with the forequarters. The thighs and buttocks are full and muscular.

Clarification:

The Pug should have large, full, and muscular thighs and buttocks, with a moderate bend of stifle and short hocks perpendicular to the ground. The hocks should not extend much beyond the point of the rump. Pugs should have strong, powerful hindquarters. Viewed from above, the rear should be approximately as wide as the shoulders.

Undesirable—Straight or exaggerated stifles, fine bone, legs too short or too long, cow hocks, toeing in or out, thin thighs, narrow rear (pear-shaped).

Coat—The coat is fine, smooth, soft, short, and glossy, neither hard nor woolly.

Clarification:
Single and double coats are both acceptable as long as they are not hard, long, or woolly. Guard hairs (when present) may be a little longer.

Color—The colors are silver, apricot-fawn, or black. The silver or apricot-fawn colors should be decided so as to make the contrast complete between the color and the trace and the mask.

Clarification:
Apricot-fawn may vary from a cream color to a deep apricot or reddish gold. Silver-fawn has a definite clear silver cast and is very rarely seen at all today. Regardless of the fawn shade, the important point is that the color be clear and distinctly contrasted with the black pigmentation of the mask and ears. A smattering of black-tipped quard hairs, hardly visible unless inspected closely, is quite common. This should not be confused with a smutty coat. Black should be very glossy, with no sign of rust or grey.

Pugs should be judged with no preference for either fawn or black coat color. An advantage of the black Pug is his silhouette. A disadvantage is the lack of distinct definition in the head, which is afforded the fawn because of the striking color contrast in mask and markings. Also, the black color gives the optical illusion of finer bone, less substance, and smaller size. For this reason, the judge must give particular attention to the black's head and substance to ascertain that all necessary qualities are present or not overlooked.

A few white hairs found on the chest of either fawn or black are permissible on an otherwise excellent specimen. As both colors age, they may develop frosting on their muzzle. This should not be penalized.

Undesirable—Fawn, smuttiness, indistinct colors, a bleeding of the black areas into the fawn, lack of distinct demarcation between black and fawn areas, broad saddles, white spots, black-grey or rusty coats.

Markings—The markings are clearly defined. The muzzle or mask, ears, moles on cheeks, thumb mark or diamond on forehead, and the back trace should be as black as possible. The mask should be black. The more intense and well defined it is, the better. The trace is a black line extending from the occiput to the tail.

Clarification:

This portion of the standard refers only to the fawn Pug. The mask should be as black as possible. There must be a distinct separation between the black marking and the fawn, not actual smutty shading from one to the other. Ears should be densely black to the base. The mole on the cheek should be noticeably black. The diamond or thumb mark that is called for in the standard is not always seen. Ideally, the fawn head wrinkles appear to be outlined in black, which sets off the thumb mark. The trace is a narrow line extending along the spine from the occiput to tail. This characteristic has largely disappeared. Today, a trace may best be defined as a definite darkening of coat color along the spine. The trace should never be confused with saddling or smut.

Gait—Viewed from the front, the forelegs should be carried well forward, showing no weakness in the pasterns, the paws landing squarely with the central toes straight ahead. The rear action should be strong and free through hocks and stifles, with no twisting or turning in or out at the joints. The hind legs should follow in line with the front. There is a slight natural convergence of the limbs both fore and aft, as speed increases. A slight roll of the hindquarters typifies the gait, which should be free, self-assured, and jaunty.

Clarification:

The Pug should be moved at a collected trot on a loose lead, as befits a companion dog. Long, sweeping strides like a sporting dog would not be characteristic of a dog with the build of a Pug.

Temperament—This is an even-tempered breed, exhibiting stability, playfulness, great charm, dignity, and an outgoing, loving disposition.

Clarification:

Pugs are outgoing, boisterous on occasion, gaily mischievous, stubborn, willful, and self-confident. The Pug is a cheerful amiable little soul who exhibits high spirits and loves to play, but is not nervous or high strung. Pugs can be good alarm dogs and are very patient with children. The exhibition of their naturally high spirits in the ring should be considered favorably, whereas indications of shyness, nervousness, and aggressiveness toward dogs or people, other than in play, are unusual and unacceptable.

Sex Differences— Although the Pug standard does not explore the differences in appearance between dogs and bitches, it should be well defined. Dogs should appear masculine and bitches feminine.

The male Pug is, on average, somewhat larger, with more bone and a larger, more wrinkled head. While bitches tend to be smaller than the dogs, they should always be in proportion, neither weedy nor lacking in head. While breed characteristics are more pronounced in the male, they should not be overdone or coarse. The bitch shows femininity without weakness or

The Pug's cheerful and patient demeanor makes him a fun and trustworthy companion for children.

over refinement. There is little difference in temperament between the male and female.

Grooming—The Pug is a natural breed, which means that very little exterior grooming is required to keep the Pug clean, neat, and in show condition. A bath, a nail clipping, a trim of the feathers along the tail and rear, if desired, and the Pug is ready for the ring. The removal of whiskers is optional. A Pug is shown in his natural state.

While the Scale of Points is no longer in the AKC standard, we feel it is useful to the breeder and the judge. It is a guide in evaluating the various aspects of the Pug. It should not be used in literal or mathematical manner to consider individual parts above the dog's overall quality. Balance, condition, and zest all contribute to make the Pug far more than merely the sum of his parts.

Scale of Points	Fawn	Black
Symmetry	10	10
Size	5	5
Condition	5	5
Body	10	10
Legs and feet	5	5
Head	5	5
Muzzle	10	10
Ears	5	5
Eyes	10	10
Mask	5	-
Wrinkles	5	5
Tail	10	10
Trace	5	-
Coat	5	5
Color	5	10
Total	100	100

THE OFFICIAL AKC STANDARD FOR THE PUG

General Appearance—Symmetry and general appearance are decidedly square and cobby. A lean, leggy Pug and a dog with short legs and a long body are equally objectionable.

Size, Proportion, Substance—The Pug should be *multum in parvo*, and this condensation (if the word may be used) is shown by compactness of form, well knit proportions, and hardness of developed muscle. Weight from 14 to 18 pounds (dog or bitch) desirable. *Proportion* square. **Head**—The *head* is large, massive, round-not apple-headed, with no indentation of the *skull*. The *eyes* are dark in color, very large, bold and prominent, globular in shape, soft and solicitous in expression, very lustrous, and, when excited, full of fire. The *ears* are thin, small, soft, like black velvet. There are two kinds-the "rose" and the "button." Preference is given to the latter. The *wrinkles* are large and deep. The *muzzle* is short, blunt, square, but not upfaced. *Bite*—A Pug's bite should be very slightly undershot.

Neck, Topline, Body—The *neck* is slightly arched. It is strong, thick, and with enough length to carry the head proudly. The 0 *back* is level from the withers to the high tail set. The *body* is short and cobby, wide in chest and well ribbed up. The *tail* is curled as tightly as possible over the hip. The double curl is perfection.

Forequarters—The *legs* are very strong, straight, of moderate length, and are set well under. The *elbows* should be directly under the withers when viewed from the side. The *shoulders* are moderately laid back. The *pasterns* are strong, neither steep nor down. The *feet* are neither so long as the foot of the hare, nor so round as that of the cat; well split-up toes, and the nails black. Dewclaws are generally removed.

Hindquarters—The strong, powerful hindquarters have moderate bend of *stifle* and short *hocks* perpendicular to the ground. The legs are parallel when viewed from behind. The hindquarters are in balance with the forequarters. The *thighs* and *buttocks* are full and muscular. Feet as in front.

Coat—The coat is fine, smooth, soft, short and glossy, neither hard nor woolly.

Color—The colors are silver, apricot-fawn, or black. The silver or apricot-fawn colors should be decided so as to make the contrast complete between the color and the trace and the mask.

Markings—The *markings* are clearly defined. The muzzle or mask, ears, moles on cheeks, thumb mark or diamond on forehead, and the back trace should be as black as possible. The mask should be black. The more intense and well defined it is, the better. The trace is a black line extending from the occiput to the tail.

Gait—Viewed from the front, the forelegs should be carried well forward, showing no weakness in the pasterns, the paws landing squarely with the central toes straight ahead. The rear action should be strong and free through hocks and stifles, with no twisting or turning in or out at the joints. The hind legs should follow in line with the front. There is a slight natural convergence of the limbs both fore and aft. A slight roll of the hindquarters typifies the gait which should be free, self-assured, and jaunty.

Temperament—This is an even-tempered breed, exhibiting stability, playfulness, great charm, dignity, and an outgoing, loving disposition.

Approved October 8, 1991
Effective November 28, 1991

TRAINING YOUR PUG

HOUSETRAINING

When it comes to training, some breeds of dog are more difficult to get the desired response from than others are. Successful training depends a great deal on just how much a dog desires his master's approval. The dog that lives to please his master will do everything in his power to gain approval. Pug owners are extremely fortunate because Pugs strive to please their masters.

Some professional dog trainers advise obtaining a puppy on the 49th day of his life, at which time a puppy is most ready to bond with a human and subsequently depend on that person for approval. After the 49th day, a puppy goes through varying stages, which make him less prone to human bonding and more independent in nature. Prior to that time, a puppy needs to be with his siblings and mother.

Although not all behaviorists will ascribe to the 49th day theory, there does seem to be general agreement that the optimum

It's important that your Pug puppy spends enough time with his mother and littermates before bringing him home. A puppy should begin to feel secure at seven or eight weeks of age.

time to bring a puppy into his new home is at about seven to eight weeks of age. It is wise to at least consider this information and discuss it with the breeder from whom you will be purchasing your puppy.

The key to having a well-trained Pug is to start play training him at a very young age. Although it's difficult to imagine that your sweet, gentle Pug traces back to the wolf, it will help you understand your dog's behavior patterns. The wolf mother plays with her cubs, and in turn teaches them what they may and may not do. The Pug puppy, like his wolf cub ancestors, must think he is having fun in order to learn.

Never allow a Pug puppy to do something that you would not want him to do as an adult. Although it may be cute now to let your puppy nip your hands or feet, refuse to give up a toy, or jump on you, allowing him to do so encourages the negative behavior, which will continue into his adulthood and be very difficult to stop.

The key to successful dog training is not to allow unacceptable behavior from the beginning. Always remember to replace the negative behavior with the correct one, using positive reinforcement.

During training, it is very important that your Pug is absolutely confident of his place in the "pack," or his human family. The Pug's position in the pecking order must be below every family member, which should clear to the dog from the first day he enters his new home.

CRATE TRAINING

Without a doubt, the best way to housetrain a Pug is to use the crate method. First-time dog owners are initially inclined to see

the crate method of housetraining as cruel, but those same people will thank me later for having suggested it in the first place. All dogs need a place of their own to retreat to and you will find that the Pug will consider his crate that place.

Using the crate reduces housetraining time and avoids keeping a puppy under constant stress by incessantly correcting him for making mistakes in the house. The anti-crate advocates consider it cruel to confine a puppy for any length of time, but they find no problem in constantly harassing and punishing the puppy when he wets the carpet or relieves himself behind the sofa.

Crate training is the fastest and easiest way to housetrain your Pug, because dogs do not want to soil where they eat and sleep.

The crate used for housetraining should only be large enough for the puppy to stand up and lie down in and stretch out comfortably. These crates are available at most pet emporiums at a wide range of prices. It is unnecessary to dash out and buy a new crate every few weeks to accommodate the Pug's rapid growth spurts. Simply cut a piece of plywood to partition off the excess space in the large crate and move it back as needed.

Begin housetraining your puppy by feeding him in his crate so that he becomes accustomed to it. Keep the door closed and latched while the puppy is eating. When the meal is finished, open the crate and carry the puppy outdoors to the spot where you want him to eliminate. Remember to use the same words consistently, for example, "go out" or "potty." It doesn't make a difference what words you choose, as long as you are consistent. The important point is that the puppy will learn both where to eliminate and that certain words mean a specific behavior is expected.

In the event that you do not have outdoor access or will be away from home for long periods of time, begin housetraining by placing newspapers in some out of the way corner that is easily accessible to the puppy. If you routinely take your puppy to the same spot, you will reinforce the habit of going there to eliminate.

It is important that you do not let the puppy run loose after eating. Young puppies will eliminate almost immediately after eating or drinking, when they first wake up, and after playing. If you keep a watchful eye on your puppy, you will quickly learn that a puppy usually circles and sniffs the floor just before he relieves himself. Do not give your puppy the opportunity to learn that he can eliminate in the house! Your housetraining chores will be reduced considerably if you avoid bad habits from beginning in the first place.

If you are unable to watch your puppy every minute, he should be in his crate with the door securely latched. Each time you put him in the crate give him a small treat of some kind. Throw the treat to the back of the crate and encourage the puppy to walk in on his own, praising him and perhaps handing him another piece of the treat through the wires of the crate.

Your puppy must learn to stay in his crate without complaining. Though it may be difficult, try not to succumb to his complaints about being in his crate. A sharp "No" and a tap on the crate will

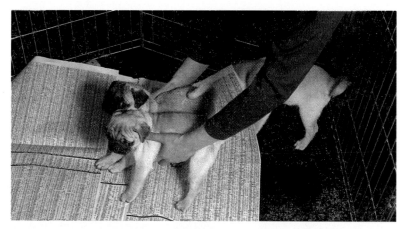

If you take your Pug puppy to the same place to eliminate every time, he'll know what is expected of him. Reinforce what he has learned by praising him when he relieves himself in the correct area.

usually get the puppy to understand that theatrics will not result in liberation.

Do understand that a puppy of 8 to 12 weeks of age will not be able to contain himself for long periods of time. Puppies of that age must relieve themselves every few hours except at night, so adjust your schedule accordingly. Also, make sure that your puppy has relieved both his bowels and bladder before bedtime.

Your first priority in the morning is to get the puppy outdoors. Just how early this ritual will take place depends more on your puppy than on you. If your Pug is like most other dogs, there will be no doubt in your mind when he needs to be let out. You will also very quickly learn to tell the difference between the "this is an emergency" complaint and the "I just want out" grumbling. Do not test the young puppy's ability to contain himself. His vocal demand to be let out is confirmation that the housetraining lesson is being learned.

If you need to be away from home all day, you cannot leave your puppy in a crate; however, do not make the mistake of allowing him to roam the house or even a large room at will. Confine the puppy to a small room or partitioned-off area and cover the floor with newspaper. Make this area large enough so that the puppy will not have to relieve himself next to his bed or

An exercise pen gives your Pug the opportunity to exercise while still keeping him safely confined.

food and water bowls. You will soon find that the puppy will be inclined to use one particular spot to relieve himself. When you are home, you must take the puppy to this exact spot to eliminate at the appropriate time.

BASIC TRAINING

Early puppy kindergarten, along with puppy play training, are vital if you plan to do obedience work of any kind. Most Pugs could easily get their Companion Dog (CD) titles if their owners put the effort into the project. Pugs are great obedience title candidates and many have won their Companion Dog Excellent

For the best results, train your Pug in a quiet and relaxing environment that is free of distractions.

(CDX) titles. A respectable number of Pugs have earned their Utility Dog (UD) title and Tora John, a Pug owned by Ruth Minge, has even acquired his Utility Dog Tracking (UDT) title.

Your mood and the environment in which you train your Pug are just as important as his state of mind at the time. Never begin training when you are irritated, distressed, or preoccupied. Nor should you begin basic training in a place that interferes with your or your dog's concentration. Once your Pug learns the commands, you can begin testing him in public places; however, it's best to first work in a quiet, private place where you can concentrate fully on each other.

Leash Training

It is never too early to accustom your Pug puppy to a collar and leash, which helps to keep him under control. Although it may not be necessary for him to wear his collar and identification tags within the confines of your home, no dog should ever leave home without a collar and without the leash held securely in your hand.

Begin getting your Pug puppy used to his collar by leaving it on for a few minutes at a time, gradually extending the time you leave it on. Most Pugs become accustomed to their collars very quickly and forget they are even wearing one. Once this is accomplished, attach a lightweight leash to the collar while you are playing with the puppy. Do not try to guide the puppy at first; the point here is to accustom him to the feeling of having something attached to the collar.

Some Pug puppies easily adapt to their collars and without any undo resistance, learn to be guided with the leash, while others adamantly refuse leash training and seem intent on strangling themselves before submitting. If your puppy is one of the latter, do not continue to force the issue. Simply create a lasso with your leash and put your Pug's head and front legs through the lasso opening so that the leash encircles his shoulders and chest, just behind the front legs. Young Pugs seem to object less to this method than having the leash around their neck.

Encourage your puppy to follow you as you move away from him. If the puppy is reluctant to cooperate, coax him along with a treat of some kind. Hold the treat in front his nose to encourage

Give your Pug puppy time to get used to the feel of a leash and collar. Once he feels comfortable, you can go anywhere without the worry of him wandering into danger.

him to follow you. Just as soon as the puppy takes a few steps toward you, praise him enthusiastically and continue to do so as you move along.

Make the initial leash session very brief and enjoyable and continue the lessons in your home or yard until the puppy is completely unconcerned about the fact that he is on a leash. With a treat in one hand and the leash in the other, you can begin to use both to guide the puppy in the direction you wish to go.

Once the puppy is used to the leash around his body and is walking with you, you can start attaching the leash to his collar. Your walks can begin in front of the house and eventually extend down the street and around the block. This is one lesson no puppy is too young to learn.

Using food treats and praise in conjunction with your training will enable your Pug to make positive associations with the basic commands.

The No Command

There is no doubt that the no command is one of the most important commands your Pug puppy will ever learn, and it's critical that he learns it as soon as possible. Remember one important piece of advice: Never give a command you are not prepared and able to follow through. The only way a puppy learns how to obey commands is to realize that once issued, they must be complied with. Learning the no command should start on the first day of the puppy's arrival at your home.

The Come Command

The come command is the next most important lesson that

your Pug puppy needs to learn. Therefore, it is very important that he learns his name as soon as possible. Constant repetition is what does the trick in teaching a puppy his name. Use the puppy's name every time you talk to him.

The come command could save your Pug's life when the two of you venture out into the world. A dog must understand and obey the come command without question, but he should not associate it with fear. Your dog's response to his name and the word "Come" should always be associated with a pleasant experience, like receiving praise and petting, or particularly in the case of the Pug, a food treat.

When training your Pug, it is far easier to avoid bad habits than it is to correct them later. Never give the come command unless you are sure that your Pug puppy will come to you. The very young puppy is far more inclined to respond to the come command than the older Pug. Use the command when the puppy is already on his way to you or give the command while walking or running away from him. Clap your hands and sound very happy and excited about having the puppy join in on this "game."

The very young Pug will normally want to stay as close to his owner as possible, especially in strange surroundings. When your puppy sees you moving away, his natural inclination will be to get close to you. This is a perfect time to use the come command.

Later, as the puppy grows more independent and headstrong, as you now know a Pug can do, you may want to attach a long leash or rope to his collar to ensure the correct response. Do not chase or punish your puppy for not obeying the come command; doing so in the initial stages of training makes the youngster associate the command with something to resist, which will result in avoidance rather than the immediate positive response that you desire. It is imperative that you praise your Pug puppy and give him a treat when he does come to you, even if he has a delayed reaction.

The Sit and Stay Commands

The sit and stay commands are just as important to your Pug's safety (and your sanity!) as the no and come commands. Even a small puppy can learn the sit command quickly, especially if you approach it like a game and a food treat is involved.

First, remember that the Pug-in-training should always have a collar and leash on for all of his training lessons. A Pug is certainly not beyond getting up and walking away when he has decided enough is enough. Give the sit command while pushing down lightly on your Pug's hindquarters. Praise the dog lavishly when he does sit. This should be accompanied by returning the dog to the desired position. Once your Pug has begun to understand the sit command, you may be able to assume the position by simply putting your hand on the dog's chest and exerting slight backward pressure.

Allow your dog to get up from the sit position only when you decide he can do so. Do not test the young Pug's patience to the limits. Remember that

Once your Pug can sit properly, teach him to remain in position until you release him.

you are dealing with a baby and the attention span of any youngster is relatively short. When you do decide that the dog can get up, call his name, say "OK," and make a big fuss over him. Praise and a food treat are in order every time your Pug responds to a command correctly.

Once your Pug has mastered the sit lesson, you may start on the stay command. With your Pug on leash and facing you, command him to sit and then take a step or two back. If he attempts to get up to follow you, firmly say, "Sit-Stay!" raising your hand, palm toward the dog, and again commanding him to "Stay!"

Any attempt on your dog's part to get up must be corrected at once. Return him to the sit position and repeat, "Stay!" Once he begins to understand what you want, you can slowly increase the distance you step back. With a long leash attached to his collar (even a clothesline will do) start with a few steps and gradually increase the distance to several yards. Your Pug must eventually learn to obey the sit/stay command, no matter how far away you are from him. Later on, with advanced training, your dog will learn that the command is to be obeyed even when you move entirely out of sight.

Avoid calling the dog to you at first, because this makes him overly anxious to get up and run to you. Until your Pug masters the sit lesson and is able to remain in the sit position for as long as you dictate, walk back to him and say "OK," which is a signal that the command is over. Later, when your dog becomes more reliable in this respect, you can call him to you.

The sit/stay lesson can take considerable time and patience, especially with the Pug puppy whose attention span is very short. It is best to keep the stay part of the lesson to a minimum until the Pug is at least five or six months old. Everything in a very young Pug's makeup will urge him to follow you wherever you go. Forcing a young puppy to operate against his natural instincts can be bewildering for him.

The Down Command

Once your Pug has mastered the sit and stay commands, you may begin work on the down, which is the single word command for lie down. Use the down command only when you want the dog to lie down. If you want your Pug to get off your sofa or to stop jumping up on people, use the off command. Do not interchange these two commands. Doing so will confuse your dog and make it nearly impossible to evoke the correct response.

The down position is especially useful if you want your Pug to remain in a particular place for a long period of time. A Pug is far more inclined to stay put when he is lying down than when he is sitting. Teaching the down command may take more time and patience than the previous lessons. It is believed by some animal behaviorists that assuming the down position somehow represents submissiveness to the dog. However, the down position seems to be more relaxing for the dog and you will find that he is less inclined to get up and wander off.

With your Pug sitting in front of and facing you, hold a treat in your right hand with the excess part of the leash in your left hand. Hold the treat under the dog's nose and slowly bring your hand down to the ground. As he follows the treat with his head and neck, give the command "Down."

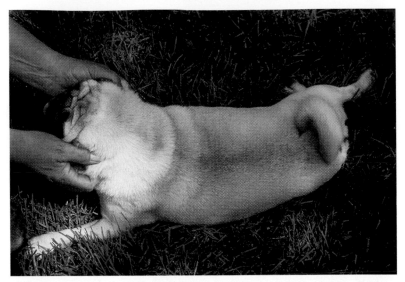

Having your Pug obey the down command easily allows you to groom him and thoroughly check his body for any lumps or abrasions.

An alternative method of getting your Pug into the down position is to move around to his right side, and as you draw his attention downward with your right hand, slide your left arm under his front legs and gently slide them forward. In the case of a small puppy, you will undoubtedly have to be on your knees next to him.

As your Pug's forelegs begin to slide out to his front, keep moving the treat along the ground until the dog's whole body is lying on the ground while you continually repeat, "Down." Once your dog has assumed the position you desire, give him the treat and a lot of praise. Continue assisting your Pug into the down position until he does so on his own, always remembering to be firm and patient.

The Heel Command

In learning to heel, your Pug will walk on your left side with his shoulder next to your leg, no matter which direction you might go or how quickly you turn. Teaching your Pug to heel will make your daily walks more enjoyable and it will make him a tractable companion when the two of you are in crowded or confusing

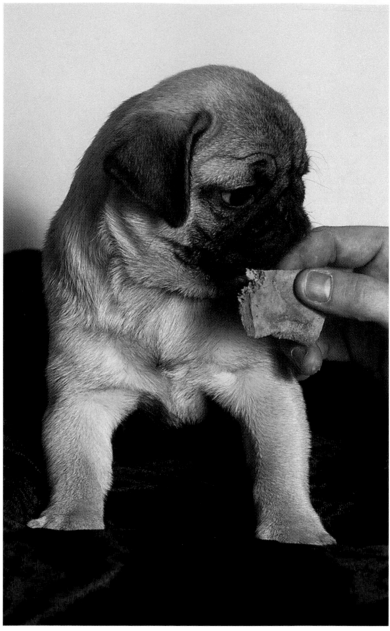

Using treats and praise will motivate your puppy during his training sessions.

situations. A Pug usually wants to be with you wherever you go, so training yours to walk along in the correct position is usually not much of a problem.

We have found that a link-chain training collar is very useful for the heeling lesson, because it provides quick pressure around the neck and a snapping sound, both of which get the dog's attention. Erroneously referred to as a "choke collar," the link-chain collar, when used properly, will not choke the dog. An employee of the pet shop at which you purchase the training collar will be able to show you the proper way to put this collar on your dog.

As you train your Pug puppy to walk along on the leash, you should accustom him to walk on your left side. The leash should cross your body from the dog's collar to your right hand. The excess portion of the leash will be folded into your right hand and your left hand on the leash will be used to make corrections with the leash.

A quick, short jerk on the leash with your left hand will keep your Pug from lunging side to side, pulling ahead, or lagging back. As you make a correction, give the "Heel" command. Always keep the leash slack as long as your dog maintains the proper position at your side.

If your dog begins to drift away, give the leash a sharp jerk, guide him back to the correct position, and give the "Heel" command. *Do not pull on the lead with steady pressure!* You must be very careful of a Pug's throat. A sharp but gentle jerking motion on the leash will get your Pug's attention. Remember to always jerk the leash and then release it.

TRAINING CLASSES

There are actually few limits to what a patient, consistent Pug owner (and the accent is most definitely on patient and consistent!) can teach his or her dog. While the Pug may not leap to perform the first time that you attempt to teach him something new, take heart. Once the lesson is mastered, your Pug will perform with enthusiasm, especially if the activity is fun and will earn him praise. Don't forget that you are dealing with what could be one of the most stubborn breeds of dog known to man; however, also be aware that the Pug is also one of the most intelligent and wonderful breeds. Your Pug performs because he wants to, not because you are *forcing* him to obey. Don't tell your Pug this, but if you are persistent enough in your training, he will eventually think the whole thing was his own idea in the first place!

For advanced obedience work beyond the basics, it is wise for the Pug owner to consider hiring a professional trainer who has long-standing experience in avoiding the pitfalls of obedience training and can help you to avoid them as well.

The new people and dogs encountered at training classes are particularly good for your Pug's socialization. There are free-of-charge classes at many parks and recreation facilities, as well as very formal, and sometimes very expensive, individual lessons with private trainers.

There are also some obedience schools that will train your Pug for you. However, unless your schedule allows no time at all to train your own dog, having someone else train him would be last on our list of recommendations. The rapport that develops between owner and dog is well worth the time and patience it requires to achieve.

If you'd like to pursue advanced obedience work with your Pug, you should consider hiring a professional trainer who has experience working with the breed to help you.

VERSATILITY

Once your Pug has been taught his basic manners, there are countless ways that the two of you can participate in enjoyable events. The breed is highly successful in conformation shows and has proven it can also do well in obedience competition. The well-trained Pug can provide a whole world of activities for the owner. You are only limited by the amount of time you wish to invest in this remarkable breed.

CANINE GOOD CITIZEN

A dog that passes a ten-part test as designated by

With the proper training and dedication, there is no limit to what your Pug can accomplish. Shown here are Jessica DiPerna and Ch. Aramis Exquisite Lucky Angel winning the Breed at CoBo Hall Dog Show.

the American Kennel Club earns the Canine Good Citizen certificate. The tests include cleanliness and grooming, socialization, obeying simple commands, and general tractability. As the name implies, any dog capable of earning the certificate can only be a better friend and companion.

THERAPY DOGS

Pugs can perform an extremely valuable service by visiting homes for the aged, orphanages, and hospitals. Pugs naturally love people and a Pug's comical expression and sparkling eyes easily charm people of all ages. It is amazing to see how kind and gentle Pugs are with small children and with ill people. It has been proven that these visits provide great therapeutic value to the patients.

SPORT of Purebred Dogs

Welcome to the exciting and sometimes frustrating sport of dogs. No doubt you are trying to learn more about dogs or you wouldn't be deep into this book. This section covers the basics that may entice you, further your knowledge and help you to understand the dog world.

Dog showing has been a very popular sport for a long time and has been taken quite seriously by some. Others only enjoy it as a hobby.

The Kennel Club in England was formed in 1859, the American Kennel Club was established in 1884, and the Canadian Kennel Club was formed in 1888. The purpose of these clubs was to register purebred dogs and maintain their Stud Books. In the beginning, the concept of registering dogs was not readily accepted. More than 36 million dogs have been enrolled in the AKC Stud Book since its inception in 1888. Presently the kennel clubs not only register dogs but adopt and enforce rules and regulations governing dog shows, obedience trials and field trials. Over the years they have fostered and encouraged interest in the health and welfare of the purebred dog. They routinely donate funds to veterinary research for study on genetic disorders.

Below are the addresses of the kennel clubs in the United States, Great Britain, and Canada.

The American Kennel Club
260 Madison Avenue
New York, NY 10016
(Their registry is located at: 5580 Centerview Drive, STE 200, Raleigh, NC 27606-3390)

The Kennel Club
1 Clarges Street
Piccadilly, London, W1Y 8AB, England

The Canadian Kennel Club
111 Eglinton Avenue
East Toronto, Ontario M6S 4V7
Canada

Today there are numerous activities that are enjoyable for both the dog and the handler. Some of the activities include conformation showing, obedience competition, tracking, agility, the Canine Good Citizen Certificate, and a wide range of instinct tests that vary from breed to breed. Where you start depends upon your goals which early on may not be readily apparent.

CONFORMATION

Conformation showing is our oldest dog show sport. This type of showing is based on the dog's appearance—that is his structure, movement, and attitude. When considering this type of showing, you need to be aware of your breed's standard and be able to evaluate your dog compared to that standard. The breeder of your puppy or other experienced breeders would be good sources for such an evaluation. Puppies can go through lots of changes over a period of time. Many puppies start out as promising hopefuls and then after maturing may be disappointing as show candidates. Even so, this should not deter them from being excellent pets.

Usually conformation training classes are offered by the local kennel or obedience clubs. These are excellent places for training puppies. The puppy should be able to walk on a lead before entering such a class. Proper ring procedure and technique for posing (stacking) the dog will be demonstrated as well as gaiting

In conformation, your Pug will be judged on his overall appearance, including structure, movement, and attitude.

91

the dog. Usually certain patterns are used in the ring such as the triangle or the "L." Conformation class, like the PKT class, will give your youngster the opportunity to socialize with different breeds of dogs and humans too.

It takes some time to learn the routine of conformation showing. Usually one starts at the puppy matches that may be AKC Sanctioned or Fun Matches. These matches are generally for puppies from two or three months to a year old, and there may be classes for the adult over the age of 12 months. Similar to point shows, the classes are divided by sex and after completion of the classes in that breed or variety, the class winners compete for Best of Breed or Variety. The winner goes on to compete in the Group and the Group winners compete for Best in Match. No championship points are awarded for match wins.

A few matches can be great training for puppies even though there is no intention to go on showing. Matches enable the puppy to meet new people and be handled by a stranger—the judge. It is also a change of environment, which broadens the horizon for both dog and handler. Matches and other dog activities boost the confidence of the handler and especially the younger handlers.

Earning an AKC championship is built on a point system, which is different from Great Britain. To become an AKC Champion of Record the dog must earn 15 points. The number of points earned each time depends upon the number of dogs in competition. The number of points available at each show depends upon the breed, its sex and the location of the show. The United States is divided into ten AKC zones. Each zone has its own set of points. The purpose of the zones is to try to equalize the points available from breed to breed and area to area. The AKC adjusts the point scale annually.

The number of points that can be won at a show are between one and five. Three-, four- and five-point wins are considered majors. Not only does the dog need 15 points won under three different judges, but those points must include two majors under two different judges. Canada also works on a point system but majors are not required.

Dogs always show before bitches. The classes available to those seeking points are: Puppy (which may be divided into 6 to 9 months and 9 to 12 months); 12 to 18 months; Novice; Bred-by-Exhibitor; American-bred; and Open. The class winners of the same sex of each breed or variety compete against each other for

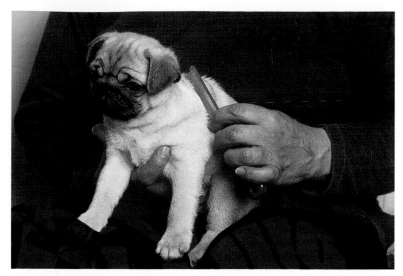

Proper grooming is essential to your Pug's success in the show ring.

Winners Dog and Winners Bitch. A Reserve Winners Dog and Reserve Winners Bitch are also awarded but do not carry any points unless the Winners win is disallowed by AKC. The Winners Dog and Bitch compete with the specials (those dogs that have attained championship) for Best of Breed or Variety, Best of Winners and Best of Opposite Sex. It is possible to pick up an extra point or even a major if the points are higher for the defeated winner than those of Best of Winners. The latter would get the higher total from the defeated winner.

At an all-breed show, each Best of Breed or Variety winner will go on to his respective Group and then the Group winners will compete against each other for Best in Show. There are seven Groups: Sporting, Hounds, Working, Terriers, Toys, Non-Sporting and Herding. Obviously there are no Groups at speciality shows (those shows that have only one breed or a show such as the American Spaniel Club's Flushing Spaniel Show, which is for all flushing spaniel breeds).

Earning a championship in England is somewhat different since they do not have a point system. Challenge Certificates are awarded if the judge feels the dog is deserving regardless of the number of dogs in competition. A dog must earn three Challenge Certificates under three different judges, with at least one of these Certificates being won after the age of 12 months. Competition is very strong and entries may be higher than they are in the U.S. The Kennel Club's Challenge Certificates are only available at Championship Shows.

In England, The Kennel Club regulations require that certain dogs, Border Collies and Gundog breeds, qualify in a working capacity (i.e., obedience or field trials) before becoming a full Champion. If they do not qualify in the working aspect, then they are designated a Show Champion, which is equivalent to the AKC's Champion of Record. A Gundog may be granted the title of Field Trial Champion (FT Ch.) if it passes all the tests in the field but would also have to qualify in conformation before becoming a full Champion. A Border Collie that earns the title of Obedience Champion (Ob Ch.) must also qualify in the conformation ring before becoming a Champion.

The US doesn't have a designation full Champion but does award for Dual and Triple Champions. The Dual Champion must be a Champion of Record, and either Champion Tracker, Herding Champion, Obedience Trial Champion or Field Champion. Any dog that has been awarded the titles of Champion of Record, and any two of the following: Champion Tracker, Herding Champion, Obedience Trial Champion, or Field Champion, may be designated as a Triple Champion.

The shows in England seem to put more emphasis on breeder judges than those in the US. There is much competition within the breeds. Therefore the quality of the individual breeds should be very good. In the United States we tend to have more "all-around judges" (those that judge multiple breeds) and use the breeder judges at the specialty shows. Breeder judges are more familiar with their own breed since they are actively breeding that breed or did so at one time. Americans emphasize Group and Best in Show wins and promote them accordingly.

The shows in England can be very large and extend over several days, with the Groups being scheduled on different days. Though multi-day shows are not common in the US, there are cluster shows, where several different clubs will use the same show site over consecutive days.

Westminster Kennel Club is our most prestigious show, although the entry is limited to 2500. In recent years, entry has been limited to Champions. This show is more formal than the majority of the shows with the judges wearing formal attire and the handlers fashionably dressed. In most instances the quality of the dogs is superb. After all, it is a show of Champions. It is a good show to study the AKC registered breeds and is by far the most exciting— especially since it is televised! WKC is one of the few shows in this country that is still benched. This means the dog must be in his benched area during the show hours except when he is being groomed, in the ring, or being exercised.

Typically, the handlers are very particular about their appearances. They are careful not to wear something that will detract from their dog but will perhaps enhance it. American ring procedure is quite formal compared to that of other countries. There is a certain

Make sure that your Pug adheres to the breed standard before entering him in competition.

etiquette expected between the judge and exhibitor and among the other exhibitors. Of course it is not always the case, but the judge is supposed to be polite, not engaging in small talk or acknowledging how well he knows the handler. There is a more informal and relaxed atmosphere at the shows in other countries. For instance, the dress code is more casual. I can see where this might be more fun for the exhibitor and especially for the novice. The US is very handler-oriented in many of the breeds. It is true, in most instances, that the experienced professional handler can present the dog better and will have a feel for what a judge likes.

In England, Crufts is The Kennel Club's own show and is most assuredly the largest dog show in the world. They've been known to have an entry of nearly 20,000, and the show lasts four days. Entry is only gained by qualifying through winning in specified classes at another Championship Show. Westminster is strictly conformation, but Crufts exhibitors and spectators enjoy not only conformation but obed-ience, agility and a multitude of exhibitions as well. Obedience was admitted in 1957 and agility in 1983.

If you are handling your own dog, please give some consideration to your apparel. For sure the dress code at matches is more informal than the point shows. However, you should wear something a little more appropriate than beach attire or ragged jeans and bare feet. If you check out the handlers and see what is presently fashionable, you'll catch on. Men usually dress with a shirt and tie and a nice sports coat. Whether you are male or female, you will want to wear comfortable clothes and shoes. You need to be able to run with your dog and you certainly don't want to take a chance of falling and hurting yourself. Heaven forbid, if nothing else, you'll upset your dog. Women usually wear a dress or two-piece outfit, preferably with pockets to carry bait, comb, brush, etc. In this case men are the lucky ones with all their pockets. Ladies, think about where your dress will be if you need to kneel on the floor and also think about running. Does it allow freedom to do so?

Showing requires dedication and preparation, but most of all it should be enjoyable for both the dog and the handler.

You need to take along dog; crate; ex pen (if you use one); extra newspaper; water pail and water; all required grooming equipment, including hair dryer and extension cord; table; chair for you; bait for dog and lunch for you and friends; and, last but not least, clean up materials, such as plastic bags, paper towels, and perhaps a bath towel and some shampoo—just in case. Don't forget your entry confirmation and directions to the show.

If you are showing in obedience, then you will want to wear pants. Many of our top obedience handlers wear pants that are color-coordinated with their

Junior Showmanship is an excellent way to build a young person's confidence in the show ring. The junior handler is judged solely on his ability and skill in presenting his dog.

dogs. The philosophy is that imperfections in the black dog will be less obvious next to your black pants.

Whether you are showing in conformation, Junior Showmanship or obedience, you need to watch the clock and be sure you are not late. It is customary to pick up your conformation armband a few minutes before the start of the class. They will not wait for you and if you are on the show grounds and not in the ring, you will upset everyone. It's a little more complicated picking up your obedience armband if you show later in the class. If you have not picked up your armband and they get to your number, you may not be allowed to show. It's best to pick up your armband early, but then you may show earlier than expected if other handlers don't pick up. Customarily all conflicts should be discussed with the judge prior to the start of the class.

Junior Showmanship

The Junior Showmanship Class is a wonderful way to build self confidence even if there are no aspirations of staying with the dog-show game later in life. Frequently, Junior Showmanship becomes the background of those who become successful exhibitors/ handlers in the future. In some instances it is taken very seriously, and success is measured in terms of wins. The Junior Handler is judged solely on his ability and skill in presenting his dog. The dog's conformation is not to be considered by the judge. Even so the condition and grooming of the dog may be a reflection upon the handler.

Usually the matches and point shows include different classes. The Junior Handler's dog may be entered in a breed or obedience class and even shown by another person in that class. Junior Showmanship classes are usually divided by age and perhaps sex. The age is determined by the handler's age on the day of the show. The classes are:

Novice Junior for those at least ten and under 14 years of age who at time of entry closing have not won three first places in a Novice Class at a licensed or member show.

Novice Senior for those at least 14 and under 18 years of age who at the time of entry closing have not won three first places in a Novice Class at a licensed or member show.

Open Junior for those at least ten and under 14 years of age who at the time of entry closing have won at least three first places in a Novice Junior Showmanship Class at a licensed or member show with competition present.

Open Senior for those at least 14 and under 18 years of age who at time of entry closing have won at least three first places in a Novice Junior Showmanship Class at a licensed or member show with competition present.

Junior Handlers must include their AKC Junior Handler number on each show entry. This needs to be obtained from the AKC.

OBEDIENCE

Obedience is necessary, without a doubt, but it can also become a wonderful hobby or even an obsession. Obedience classes and competition can provide wonderful companionship, not only with your dog but with your classmates or fellow competitors. It is always gratifying to discuss your dog's problems with others who have had similar experiences. The AKC acknowledged Obedience around 1936, and it has changed tremendously even though many of the exercises are basically the same. Today, obedience competition is just that—very competitive.

Even so, it is possible for every obedience exhibitor to come home a winner (by earning qualifying scores) even though he/she may not earn a placement in the class.

Most of the obedience titles are awarded after earning three qualifying scores (legs) in the appropriate class under three different judges. These classes offer a perfect score of 200, which is extremely rare. Each of the class exercises has its own point value. A leg is earned after receiving a score of at least 170 and at least 50 percent of the points available in each exercise. The titles are:

Companion Dog–CD
This is called the Novice Class and the exercises are:
1. Heel on leash and figure 8 .... 40 points
2. Stand for examination .... 30 points
3. Heel free .... 40 points
4. Recall .... 30 points
5. Long sit–one minute .... 30 points
6. Long down–three minutes .... 30 points
Maximum total score .... 200 points

Companion Dog Excellent–CDX
This is the Open Class and the exercises are:
1. Heel off leash and figure 8 .... 40 points
2. Drop on recall .... 30 points
3. Retrieve on flat .... 20 points
4. Retrieve over high jump .... 30 points
5. Broad jump .... 20 points
6. Long sit–three minutes (out of sight) .... 30 points
7. Long down–five minutes (out of sight) .... 30 points
Maximum total score .... 200 points

Utility Dog–UD
The Utility Class exercises are:
1. Signal Exercise .... 40 points
2. Scent discrimination-Article 1 .... 30 points
3. Scent discrimination-Article 2 .... 30 points
4. Directed retrieve .... 30 points
5. Moving stand and examination .... 30 points
6. Directed jumping .... 40 points
Maximum total score .... 200 points

After achieving the UD title, you may feel inclined to go after the UDX and/or OTCh. The UDX (Utility Dog Excellent) title went into effect in January 1994. It is not easily attained. The title requires qualifying simultaneously ten times in Open B and Utility B but not necessarily at consecutive shows.

The OTCh. (Obedience Trial Champion) is awarded after the dog has earned his UD and then goes on to earn 100 championship points, a first place in Utility, a first place in Open and another first place in either class. The placements must be won under three different judges at all-breed obedience trials. The points are determined by the number of dogs competing in the Open B and Utility B classes. The OTCh. title precedes the dog's name.

Obedience matches (AKC Sanctioned, Fun, and Show and Go) are usually available. Usually they are sponsored by the local obedience clubs. When preparing an obedience dog for a title, you will find matches very helpful. Fun Matches and Show and Go Matches are more lenient in allowing you to make corrections in the ring. This type of training is usually very necessary for the Open and Utility Classes. AKC Sanctioned Obedience Matches do not allow corrections in the ring since they must abide by the AKC Obedience Regulations. If you are interested in showing in obedience, then you should contact the AKC for a copy of the Obedience Regulations.

TRACKING

Tracking is officially classified obedience. There are three tracking titles available: Tracking Dog (TD), Tracking Dog Excellent (TDX), Variable Surface Tracking (VST). If all three tracking titles are obtained, then the dog officially becomes a CT (Champion Tracker). The CT will go in front of the dog's name.

A TD may be earned anytime and does not have to follow the other obedience titles. There are many exhibitors that prefer tracking to obedience, and there are others who do both.

Tracking Dog–TD

A dog must be certified by an AKC tracking judge that he is ready to perform in an AKC test. The AKC can provide the names of tracking judges in your area that you can contact for certification. Depending on where you live, you may have to travel a distance if there is no local tracking judge. The certification track will be equivalent to a regular AKC track. A regulation track must be 440 to 500 yards long with at least two right-angle turns out in the open. The track will be aged 30 minutes to two hours. The handler has two starting flags at the beginning of the track to indicate the direction started. The dog works on a harness and 40-foot lead and must work at least 20 feet in front of the handler. An article (either a dark glove or wallet) will be dropped at the end of the track, and the dog must indicate it but not necessarily retrieve it.

People always ask what the dog tracks. Initially, the beginner on the short-aged track tracks the tracklayer. Eventually the dog learns to track the disturbed vegetation and learns to differentiate between tracks. Getting started with tracking requires reading the AKC regulations and a good book on tracking plus finding other tracking enthusiasts. Work on the buddy system. That is—lay tracks for each other so you can practice blind tracks. It is possible to train on your own, but if you are a beginner, it is a lot more entertaining to track with a buddy. It's rewarding seeing the dog use his natural ability.

Versatile and enthusiastic, Pugs excel at a variety of activities when properly trained.

Performance tests, like tracking, allow dogs to apply their natural talents to the show ring.

Tracking Dog Excellent–TDX

The TDX track is 800 to 1000 yards long and is aged three to five hours. There will be five to seven turns. An article is left at the starting flag, and three other articles must be indicated on the track. There is only one flag at the start, so it is a blind start. Approximately one and a half hours after the track is laid, two tracklayers will cross over the track at two different places to test the dog's ability to stay with the original track. There will be at least two obstacles on the track such as a change of cover, fences, creeks, ditches, etc. The dog must have a TD before entering a TDX. There is no certification required for a TDX.

Variable Surface Tracking–VST

This test came into effect September 1995. The dog must have a TD earned at least six months prior to entering this test. The track is 600 to 800 yards long and shall have a minimum of three different surfaces. Vegetation shall be included along with two areas devoid of vegetation such as concrete, asphalt, gravel, sand, hard pan or mulch. The areas devoid of vegetation shall comprise at least one-third to one-half of the track. The track is aged three to five hours. There will be four to eight turns and four numbered articles including one leather, one plastic, one metal and one fabric dropped on the track. There is one starting flag. The handler will work at least 10 feet from the dog.

Agility

Agility was first introduced by John Varley in England at the Crufts Dog Show, February 1978, but Peter Meanwell, competitor and judge, actually developed the idea. It was officially recognized in the early 80s. Agility is extremely popular in England and Canada and growing in popularity in the U.S. The AKC acknowledged agility in August 1994. Dogs must be at least 12 months of age to be entered. It is a fascinating sport that the dog, handler and spectators enjoy to the utmost. Agility is a spectator sport! The dog performs off lead. The handler either runs with his dog or positions himself on the course and directs his dog with verbal and hand signals over a timed course over or through a variety of obstacles including a time out or pause. One of the main drawbacks to agility is finding a place to train. The obstacles take up a lot of space and it is very time consuming to put up and take down courses.

The titles earned at AKC agility trials are Novice Agility Dog (NAD), Open Agility Dog (OAD), Agility Dog Excellent (ADX), and Master Agility Excellent (MAX). In order to acquire an agility title, a dog must earn a qualifying score in its respective class on three separate occasions under two different judges. The MAX will be awarded after earning ten qualifying scores in the Agility Excellent Class.

General Information

Obedience, tracking and agility allow the purebred dog with an Indefinite Listing Privilege (ILP) number or a limited registration to be exhibited and earn titles. Application must be made to the AKC for an ILP number.

The American Kennel Club publishes a monthly *Events* magazine that is part of the *Gazette*, their official journal for the sport of purebred dogs. The *Events* section lists upcoming shows and the secretary or superintendent for them. The majority of the conformation shows in the US are overseen by licensed superintendents. Generally the entry closing date is approximately two-and-a-half weeks before the actual show. Point shows are fairly expensive, while the match shows cost about one third of the point show entry fee. Match shows usually take entries the day of the show but some are pre-entry. The best way to find match show information is through your local kennel club. Upon asking, the AKC can provide you with a list of superintendents, and you can write and ask to be put on their mailing lists.

Obedience trial and tracking test information is available through the AKC. Frequently these events are not superintended, but put on by the host club. Therefore you would make the entry with the event's secretary.

As you have read, there are numerous activities you can share with your dog. Regardless what you do, it does take teamwork. Your dog can only benefit from your attention and training. We hope this chapter has enlightened you and hope, if nothing else, you will attend a show here and there. Perhaps you will start with a puppy kindergarten class, and who knows where it may lead!

HEALTH CARE

V eterinary medicine has become far more sophisticated than what was available to our ancestors. This can be attributed to the increase in household pets and consequently the demand for better care for them. Also human medicine has become far more complex. Today diagnostic testing in veterinary medicine parallels human diagnostics. Because of better technology we can expect our pets to live healthier lives thereby increasing their life spans.

The First Checkup

You will want to take your new puppy/dog in for his first checkup within 48 to 72 hours after acquiring it. Many breeders strongly recommend this checkup and so do the humane shelters. A puppy/dog can appear healthy but he may have a serious problem that is not apparent to the layman. Most pets have some type of a minor flaw that may never cause a real problem.

Unfortunately if he/she should have a serious problem, you will want to consider the consequences of keeping the pet and the attachments that will be formed, which may be broken prematurely. Keep in mind there are many healthy dogs looking for good homes.

This first checkup is a good time to establish

It's a good idea to take your Pug puppy to the vet within 48 to 72 hours after acquiring him. He should also have regular checkups throughout his lifetime to maintain good health.

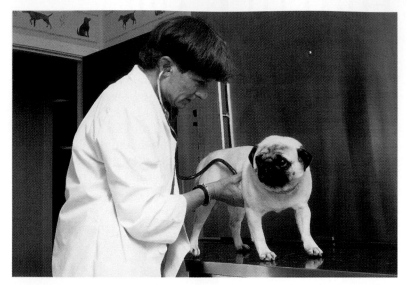

On the initial visit, your vet should discuss with you the proper diet for your Pug. If she suggests changing the dog's original diet, do so gradually to avoid stomach upset.

yourself with the veterinarian and learn the office policy regarding their hours and how they handle emergencies. Usually the breeder or another conscientious pet owner is a good reference for locating a capable veterinarian. You should be aware that not all veterinarians give the same quality of service. Please do not make your selection on the least expensive clinic, as they may be short changing your pet. There is the possibility that eventually it will cost you more due to improper diagnosis, treatment, etc. If you are selecting a new veterinarian, feel free to ask for a tour of the clinic. You should inquire about making an appointment for a tour since all clinics are working clinics, and therefore may not be available all day for sightseers. You may worry less if you see where your pet will be spending the day if he ever needs to be hospitalized.

THE PHYSICAL EXAM

Your veterinarian will check your pet's overall condition, which includes listening to the heart; checking the respiration; feeling the abdomen, muscles and joints; checking the mouth, which includes the gum color and signs of gum disease along with plaque buildup; checking the ears for signs of an infection or ear mites; examining the eyes; and, last but not least, checking the condition of the skin and coat.

He should ask you questions regarding your pet's eating and elimination habits and invite you to relay your questions. It is a good idea to prepare a list so as not to forget anything. He should discuss the proper diet and the quantity to be fed. If this should differ from your breeder's recommendation, then you should convey to him the breeder's choice and see if he approves. If he recommends changing the diet, then this should be done over a few days so as not to cause a gastrointestinal upset. It is customary to take in a fresh stool sample (just a small amount) for a test for intestinal parasites. It must be fresh, preferably within 12 hours, since the eggs hatch quickly and after hatching will not be observed under the microscope. If your pet isn't obliging then, usually the technician can take one in the clinic.

IMMUNIZATIONS

It is important that you take your puppy/dog's vaccination record with you on your first visit. In case of a puppy, presumably the breeder has seen to the vaccinations up to the time you acquired custody. Veterinarians differ in their vaccination protocol. It is not unusual for your puppy to have received vaccinations for

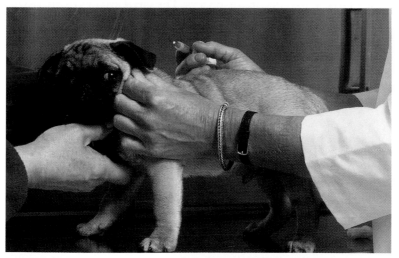

Maintaining your Pug's immunization schedule and booster shots will help him live a long and healthy life.

distemper, hepatitis, leptospirosis, parvovirus and parainfluenza every two to three weeks from the age of five or six weeks. Usually this is a combined injection and is typically called the DHLPP. The DHLPP is given through at least 12 to 14 weeks of age, and it is customary to continue with another parvovirus vaccine at 16 to 18 weeks. You may wonder why so many immunizations are necessary. No one knows for sure when the puppy's maternal antibodies are gone, although it is customarily accepted that distemper antibodies are gone by 12 weeks. Usually parvovirus antibodies are gone by 16 to 18 weeks of age. However, it is possible for the maternal antibodies to be gone at a much earlier age or even a later age. Therefore immunizations are started at an early age. The vaccine will not give immunity as long as there are maternal antibodies.

The rabies vaccination is given at three or six months of age depending on your local laws. A vaccine for bordetella (kennel cough) is advisable and can be given anytime from the age of five weeks. The coronavirus is not commonly given unless there is a problem locally. The Lyme vaccine is necessary in endemic areas. Lyme disease has been reported in 47 states.

Distemper

This is virtually an incurable disease. If the dog recovers, he is subject to severe nervous disorders. The virus attacks every tissue in the body and resembles a bad cold with a fever. It can cause a runny nose and eyes and cause gastrointestinal disorders, including a poor appetite, vomiting and diarrhea. The virus is carried by raccoons, foxes, wolves, mink and other dogs. Unvaccinated youngsters and senior citizens are very susceptible. This is still a common disease.

Hepatitis

This is a virus that is most serious in very young dogs. It is spread by contact with an infected animal or its stool or urine. The virus affects the liver and kidneys and is characterized by high fever, depression and lack of appetite. Recovered animals may be afflicted with chronic illnesses.

Leptospirosis

This is a bacterial disease transmitted by contact with the urine of an infected dog, rat or other wildlife. It produces severe symptoms of fever, depression, jaundice and internal bleeding and was fatal before the vaccine was developed. Recovered dogs can be carriers, and the disease can be transmitted from dogs to humans.

Parvovirus

This was first noted in the late 1970s and is still a fatal disease. However, with proper vaccinations, early diagnosis and prompt treatment, it is a manageable disease. It attacks the bone marrow and intestinal tract. The symptoms include depression, loss of appetite, vomiting, diarrhea and collapse. Immediate medical attention is of the essence.

Keeping your Pug safely contained while outside will prevent him from coming into contact with anything dangerous.

Rabies

This is shed in the saliva and is carried by raccoons, skunks, foxes, other dogs and cats. It attacks nerve tissue, resulting in paralysis and death. Rabies can be transmitted to people and is virtually always fatal. This disease is reappearing in the suburbs.

Bordetella (Kennel Cough)

The symptoms are coughing, sneezing, hacking and retching accompanied by nasal discharge usually lasting from a few days to several weeks. There are several disease-producing organisms responsible for this disease. The present vaccines are helpful but do not protect for all the strains. It usually is not life threatening but in some instances it can progress to a serious bronchopneumonia. The disease is highly contagious. The

Bordetella attached to canine cilia. Otherwise known as kennel cough, this disease is highly contagious and should be vaccinated against routinely.

vaccination should be given routinely for dogs that come in contact with other dogs, such as through boarding, training class or visits to the groomer.

Coronavirus

This is usually self limiting and not life threatening. It was first noted in the late '70s about a year before parvovirus. The virus produces a yellow/brown stool and there may be depression, vomiting and diarrhea.

Lyme Disease

This was first diagnosed in the United States in 1976 in Lyme, CT in people who lived in close proximity to the deer tick. Symptoms may include acute lameness, fever, swelling of joints and loss of appetite. Your veterinarian can advise you if you live in an endemic area.

After your puppy has completed his puppy vaccinations, you will continue to booster the DHLPP once a year. It is customary to booster the rabies one year after the first vaccine and then, depending on where you live, it should be boostered every year or every three years. This depends on your local laws. The Lyme and corona vaccines are boostered annually and it is recommended that the bordetella be boostered every six to eight months.

ANNUAL VISIT

I would like to impress the importance of the annual checkup, which would include the booster vaccinations, check for intestinal parasites and test for heartworm. Today in our very busy world it is rush, rush and see "how much you can get for how little." Unbelievably, some non-veterinary businesses have entered into the vaccination business. More harm than good can come to your dog through improper vaccinations, possibly from inferior vaccines and/or the wrong schedule. More than likely you truly care about your companion dog and over the years you have devoted much time and expense to his well being. Perhaps you are unaware that a vaccination is not just a vaccination. There is more involved. Please, please follow through with regular physical examinations. It is so important for your veterinarian to know your dog and this is especially true during middle age through the geriatric years. More than likely your older dog will require more than one physical a year. The annual physical is good preventive medicine. Through early diagnosis and subsequent treatment your dog can maintain a longer and better quality of life.

INTESTINAL PARASITES

Hookworms

These are almost microscopic intestinal worms that can cause anemia and therefore serious problems, including death, in young puppies. Hookworms can be transmitted to humans through penetration of the skin. Puppies may be born with them.

Roundworms

These are spaghetti-like worms that can cause a potbellied appearance and dull coat along with more severe symptoms, such as vomiting, diarrhea and coughing. Puppies acquire these while in the mother's uterus and through lactation. Both hookworms and roundworms may be acquired through ingestion.

Whipworms

These have a three-month life cycle and are not acquired through the dam. They cause intermittent diarrhea usually with mucus. Whipworms are possibly the most difficult worm to eradicate. Their eggs are very resistant to most environmental factors and can last for years until the proper conditions enable them to mature. Whipworms are seldom seen in the stool.

Intestinal parasites are more prevalent in some areas than others. Climate, soil, and contamination are big factors contributing to the incidence of intestinal parasites. Eggs are passed in the stool, lay on the ground and then become infective in a certain number of days. Each of the above worms has a different life cycle. Your best chance of becoming and remaining worm-free is to always pooper-scoop your yard. A fenced-in yard keeps stray dogs out, which is certainly helpful.

As your dog ages, his health needs will change. Keep veterinary visits regular and all vaccines up to date.

I would recommend having a fecal examination on your dog twice a year or more often if there is a problem. If your dog has a positive fecal sample, then he will be given the appropriate medication and you will be asked to bring back another stool sample in a certain period of time (depending on the type of worm) and then be rewormed. This process goes on until he has at least two negative samples. The different types of worms require different medications. You will be wasting your money and doing your dog an injustice by buying over-the-counter medication without first consulting your veterinarian.

OTHER INTERNAL PARASITES

Coccidiosis and Giardiasis

These protozoal infections usually affect puppies, especially in places where large numbers of puppies are brought together. Older dogs may harbor these infections but do not show signs unless they are stressed. Symptoms include diarrhea, weight loss and lack of appetite. These infections are not always apparent in the fecal examination.

Tapeworms

Seldom apparent on fecal floatation, they are diagnosed frequently as rice-like segments around the dog's anus and the base of the tail. Tapeworms are long, flat and ribbon like, sometimes several feet in length, and made up of many segments about five-eighths of an inch long. The two most common types of tapeworms found in the dog are:

(1) First the larval form of the flea tapeworm parasite must mature in an intermediate host, the flea, before it can become infective. Your dog acquires this by ingesting the flea through licking and chewing.

(2) Rabbits, rodents and certain large game animals serve as intermediate hosts for other species of tapeworms. If your dog should eat one of these infected hosts, then he can acquire tapeworms.

HEARTWORM DISEASE

This is a worm that resides in the heart and adjacent blood vessels of the lung that produces microfilaria, which circulate in

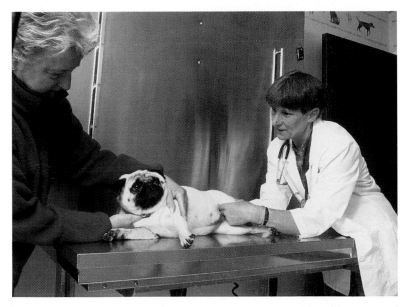

The importance of consulting a veterinarian on the diagnosis of internal disorders cannot be stressed enough—a relatively common problem could also be a sign of something more serious.

113

the bloodstream. It is possible for a dog to be infected with any number of worms from one to a hundred that can be 6 to 14 inches long. It is a life-threatening disease, expensive to treat and easily prevented. Depending on where you live, your veterinarian may recommend a preventive year-round and either an annual or semiannual blood test. The most common preventive is given once a month.

EXTERNAL PARASITES

Fleas

These pests are not only the dog's worst enemy but also enemy to the owner's pocketbook. Preventing is less expensive than treating, but regardless we'd prefer to spend our money elsewhere. Likely, the majority of our dogs are allergic to the bite of a flea, and in many cases it only takes one flea bite. The protein in the flea's saliva is the culprit. Allergic dogs have a reaction, which usually results in a "hot spot." More than likely such a reaction will involve a trip to the veterinarian for treatment. Yes, prevention is less expensive. Fortunately today there are several good products available.

Check your Pug's coat for parasites like fleas and ticks after he has been playing outside.

If there is a flea infestation, no one product is going to correct the problem. Not only will the dog require treatment so will the environment. In general flea collars are not very effective although there is now available an "egg" collar that will kill the eggs on the dog. Dips are the most economical but they are messy. There are some effective shampoos and treatments available through pet shops and veterinarians. An oral tablet arrived on the American market in 1995 and was popular in Europe the previous year. It sterilizes the female flea but will not kill adult fleas. Therefore the tablet, which is given monthly, will decrease the flea population but is not a "cure-all." Those dogs that suffer from flea-bite allergy will still be subjected to the bite of the flea. Another popular parasiticide is permethrin, which is applied to the back of the dog in one or two places depending on the dog's weight. This product works as a repellent causing the flea to get "hot feet" and jump off. Do not confuse this product with some of the organophosphates that are also applied to the dog's back.

Some products are not usable on young puppies. Treating fleas should be done under your veterinarian's guidance. Frequently it is necessary to combine products and the layman does not have the knowledge regarding possible toxicities. It is hard to believe but there are a few dogs that do have a natural resistance to fleas. Nevertheless it would be wise to treat all pets at the same time. Don't forget your cats. Cats just love to prowl the neighborhood and consequently return with unwanted guests.

Adult fleas live on the dog but their eggs drop off the dog into the environment. There they go through four larval stages before reaching adulthood, and thereby are able to jump back on the poor unsuspecting dog. The cycle resumes and takes between 21 to 28 days under ideal conditions. There are environmental products available that will kill both the adult fleas and the larvae.

Ticks

Ticks carry Rocky Mountain Spotted Fever, Lyme disease, and can cause tick paralysis. They should be removed with tweezers, trying to pull out the head. The jaws carry disease. There is a tick preventive collar that does an excellent job. The ticks automatically back out on those dogs wearing collars.

Sarcoptic Mange

This is a mite that is difficult to find on skin scrapings. The pinnal reflex is a good indicator of this disease. Rub the ends of the pinna (ear) together and the dog will start scratching with his foot. Sarcoptes are highly contagious to other dogs and to humans although they do not live long on humans. They cause intense itching.

Most breeders will ask that you have your pet spayed or neutered. Breeding requires a great deal of knowledge about the breed and should not be taken lightly.

Demodectic Mange

This is a mite that is passed from the dam to her puppies. It affects youngsters age three to ten months. Diagnosis is confirmed by skin scraping. Small areas of alopecia around the eyes, lips and/ or forelegs become visible. There is little itching unless there is a secondary bacterial infection. Some breeds are afflicted more than others.

Cheyletiella

This causes intense itching and is diagnosed by skin scraping. It lives in the outer layers of the skin of dogs, cats, rabbits and humans. Yellow-gray scales may be found on the back and the rump, top of the head and the nose.

TO BREED OR NOT TO BREED

More than likely your breeder has requested that you have your puppy neutered or spayed. Your breeder's request is based on what is healthiest for your dog and what is most beneficial for your breed. Experienced and conscientious breeders devote many years into developing a bloodline. In order to do this, he makes every effort to plan each breeding in regard to conformation, temperament and health. This type of breeder does his best to perform the necessary testing (i.e., OFA, CERF, testing for inherited blood disorders, thyroid, etc.). Testing is expensive and sometimes very disheartening when a favorite dog doesn't pass his health tests. The health history pertains not only to the breeding stock but to the immediate ancestors. Reputable breeders do not want their offspring to be bred indiscriminately. Therefore you may be asked to neuter or spay your puppy. Of course there is always the exception, and your breeder may agree to let you breed your dog under his direct supervision. This is an important concept. More and more effort is being made to breed healthier dogs.

Spay/Neuter

There are numerous benefits of performing this surgery at six months of age. Unspayed females are subject to mammary and ovarian cancer. In order to prevent mammary cancer she must be spayed prior to her first heat cycle. Later in life, an unspayed female may develop a pyometra (an infected uterus), which is definitely life threatening.

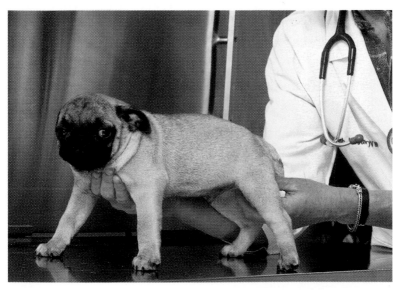

Spaying or neutering your dog can decrease his or her chances of developing cancers of the reproductive organs.

Breeding only the best-quality dogs ensures that the Pug will stay free of hereditary diseases.

Spaying is performed under a general anesthetic and is easy on the young dog. As you might expect it is a little harder on the older dog, but that is no reason to deny her the surgery. The surgery removes the ovaries and uterus. It is important to remove all the ovarian tissue. If some is left behind, she could remain attractive to males. In order to view the ovaries, a reasonably long incision is necessary. An ovariohysterectomy is considered major surgery.

Neutering the male at a young age will inhibit some characteristic male behavior that owners frown upon. Some boys will not hike their legs and mark territory if they are neutered at six months of age. Also neutering at a young age has hormonal benefits, lessening the chance of hormonal aggressiveness.

Surgery involves removing the testicles but leaving the scrotum. If there should be a retained testicle, then he definitely needs to be neutered before the age of two or three years. Retained testicles can develop into cancer. Unneutered males are at risk for testicular cancer, perineal fistulas, perianal tumors and fistulas and prostatic disease.

Intact males and females are prone to housebreaking accidents. Females urinate frequently before, during and after heat cycles, and males tend to mark territory if there is a female in heat. Males may show the same behavior if there is a visiting dog or guests.

Surgery involves a sterile operating procedure equivalent to human surgery. The incision site is shaved, surgically scrubbed and draped. The veterinarian wears a sterile surgical gown, cap, mask and gloves. Anesthesia should be monitored by a registered technician. It is customary for the veterinarian to recommend a pre-anesthetic blood screening, looking for metabolic problems and a ECG rhythm strip to check for normal heart function. Today anesthetics are equal to human anesthetics, which enables your dog to walk out of the clinic the same day as surgery.

Some folks worry about their dog gaining weight after being neutered or spayed. This is usually not the case. It is true that some dogs may be less active so they could develop a problem, but most dogs are just as active as they were before surgery. However, if your dog should begin to gain, then you need to decrease his food and see to it that he gets a little more exercise.

MEDICAL PROBLEMS

Anal Sacs

These are small sacs on either side of the rectum that can cause the dog discomfort when they are full. They should empty when the dog has a bowel movement. Symptoms of inflammation or impaction are excessive licking under the tail and/or a bloody or sticky discharge from the anal area. Breeders like myself recommend emptying the sacs on a regular schedule when bathing the dog. Many veterinarians prefer this isn't done unless there are symptoms. You can express the sacs by squeezing the two sacs (at the five and seven o'clock positions) in and up toward the anus. Take precautions not to get in the way of the foul-smelling fluid that is expressed. Some dogs object to this procedure so it would be wise to have someone hold the head. Scooting is caused by anal-sac irritation and not worms.

Colitis

The stool may be frank blood or blood tinged and is the result of inflammation of the colon. Colitis, sometimes intermittent, can be the result of stress, undiagnosed whipworms, or perhaps idiopathic (no explainable reason). If intermittent bloody stools are an ongoing problem, you should probably feed a diet higher in fiber. Seek professional help if your dog feels poorly and/or the condition persists.

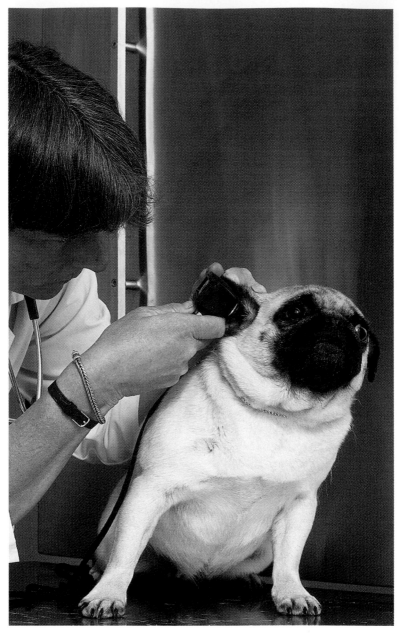

Ear care should not be taken lightly. Ask your veterinarian to explain the proper way to care for your Pug's ears.

Conjunctivitis

Many breeds are prone to this problem. The conjunctiva is the pink tissue that lines the inner surface of the eyeball except the clear, transparent cornea. Irritating substances such as bacteria, foreign matter or chemicals can cause it to become reddened and swollen. It is important to keep any hair trimmed from around the eyes. Long hair stays damp and aggravates the problem. Keep the eyes cleaned with warm water and wipe away any matter that has accumulated in the corner of the eyes. If the condition persists, you should see your veterinarian. This problem goes hand in hand with keratoconjunctivitis sicca.

Ear Infection

Otitis externa is an inflammation of the external ear canal that begins at the outside opening of the ear and extends inward to the eardrum. Dogs with pendulous ears are prone to this disease, but isn't it interesting that breeds with upright ears also have a high incidence of problems? Allergies, food and inhalent, along with hormonal problems, such as hypothyroidism, are major contributors to the disease. For those dogs which have recurring problems you need to investigate the underlying cause if you hope to cure them.

Be careful never to get water into the ears. Water provides a great medium for bacteria to grow. If your dog swims or you inadvertently get water into his ears, then use a drying agent. An at-home preparation would be to use equal parts of three-percent hydrogen peroxide and 70-percent rubbing alcohol. Another preparation is equal parts of white vinegar and water. Your veterinarian alternatively can provide a suitable product. When cleaning the ears, be careful of using cotton tip applicators since they make it easy to pack debris down into the canal. Only clean what you can see.

If your dog has an ongoing infection, don't be surprised if your veterinarian recommends sedating him and flushing his ears with a bulb syringe. Sometimes this needs to be done a few times to get the ear clean. The ear must be clean so that medication can come in contact with the canal. Be prepared to return for rechecks until the infection is gone. This may involve more flushings if the ears are very bad.

For chronic or recurring cases, your veterinarian may recommend thyroid testing, etc., and a hypoallergenic diet for a trial period of 10 to 12 weeks. Depending on your dog, it may be a good idea to see a dermatologist. Ears shouldn't be taken lightly. If the condition gets out of hand, then surgery may be necessary. Please ask your veterinarian to explain proper ear maintenance for your dog.

Flea Bite Allergy

This is the result of a hypersensitivity to the bite of a flea and its saliva. It only takes one bite to cause the dog to chew or scratch himself raw. Your dog may need medical attention to ease his discomfort. You need to clip the hair around the "hot spot" and wash it with a mild soap and water and you may need to do this daily if the area weeps. Apply an antibiotic anti-inflammatory product. Hot spots can occur from other trauma, such as grooming.

Interdigital Cysts

Check for these on your dog's feet if he shows signs of lameness. They are frequently associated with staph infections and can be quite painful. A home remedy is to soak the infected foot in a solution of a half teaspoon of bleach in a couple of quarts of water. Do this two to three times a day for a couple of days. Check with your veterinarian for an alternative remedy; antibiotics usually work well. If there is a recurring problem, surgery may be required.

Lameness

It may only be an interdigital cyst or it could be a mat between the toes, especially if your dog licks his feet. Sometimes it is hard to determine which leg is affected. If he is holding up his leg, then you need to see your veterinarian.

Skin

Frequently poor skin is the result of an allergy to fleas, an inhalant allergy or food allergy. These types of problems usually result in a staph dermatitis. Dogs with food allergy usually show signs of severe itching and scratching. Some dogs with food allergies never once itch. Their only symptom is swelling of the ears with no ear infection. Food allergy may result in recurrent bacterial skin and ear infections. Your veterinarian or dermatologist will recommend a good restricted diet. It is not wise for you to hit and miss with different dog foods. Many of the diets offered over

A skin disorder could be the result of a food allergy. Consult your vet if your Pug suffers from severe scratching and itching.

the counter are not the hypoallergenic diet you are led to believe. Dogs acquire allergies through exposure.

Inhalant allergies result in atopy, which causes licking of the feet, scratching the body and rubbing the muzzle. It may be seasonable. Your veterinarian or dermatologist can perform intradermal testing for inhalant allergies. If your dog should test positive, then a vaccine may be prepared. The results are very satisfying.

Tonsillitis

Usually young dogs have a higher incidence of this problem than the older ones. The older dogs have built up resistance. It is very contagious. Sometimes it is difficult to determine if it is tonsillitis or kennel cough since the symptoms are similar. Symptoms include fever, poor eating, swallowing with difficulty and retching up a white, frothy mucus.

As a Pug owner, you are responsible for knowing about the medical conditions that can affect the breed.

DENTAL CARE for Your Dog's Life

So you've got a new puppy! You also have a new set of puppy teeth in your household. Anyone who has ever raised a puppy is abundantly aware of these new teeth. Your puppy will chew anything it can reach, chase your shoelaces, and play "tear the rag" with any piece of clothing it can find. When puppies are newly born, they have no teeth. At about four weeks of age, puppies of most breeds begin to develop their deciduous or baby teeth. They begin eating semi-solid food, fighting and biting with their litter mates, and learning discipline from their mother. As their new teeth come in, they inflict more pain on their mother's breasts, so her feeding sessions become less frequent and shorter. By six or eight weeks, the mother will start growling to warn her pups when they are fighting too roughly or hurting her as they nurse too much with their new teeth.

Puppies need to chew. It is a necessary part of their physical and mental development. They develop muscles and necessary

Safe chew toys are excellent tools to relieve your Pug's need to chew and to keep his teeth and jaw occupied.

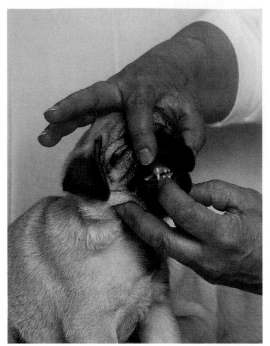

Your dog's oral care is just as important as his grooming or nutritional needs. Have his teeth checked once a year by your vet.

life skills as they drag objects around, fight over possession, and vocalize alerts and warnings. Puppies chew on things to explore their world. They are using their sense of taste to determine what is food and what is not. How else can they tell an electrical cord from a lizard? At about four months of age, most puppies begin shedding their baby teeth. Often these teeth need some help to come out and make way for the permanent teeth. The incisors (front teeth) will be replaced first. Then, the adult canine or fang teeth erupt. When the baby tooth is not shed before the permanent tooth comes in, veterinarians call it a retained deciduous tooth. This condition will often cause gum infections by trapping hair and debris between the permanent tooth and the retained baby tooth. Puppies that have adequate chew toys will have less destructive behavior, develop more physically, and have less chance of retained deciduous teeth.

During the first year, your dog should be seen by your veterinarian at regular intervals. Your veterinarian will let you know when to bring in your puppy for vaccinations and parasite examinations. At each visit, your veterinarian should inspect the lips, teeth, and mouth as part of a complete physical examination. You should take some part in the maintenance of your dog's oral health. You should examine your dog's mouth weekly throughout his first year to make sure there are no sores, foreign objects, tooth problems, etc. If your dog drools excessively, shakes its head, or has bad breath, consult your veterinarian. By the time your dog is six months old, the permanent teeth are all in and plaque can start to accumulate on the tooth surfaces. This is when your dog needs to develop good dental-care habits to prevent calculus build-up on its teeth. Brushing is best. That is a fact that cannot be denied. However, some dogs do not like their teeth brushed regularly, or you may not be able to accomplish the task. In that case, you should consider a product that will help prevent plaque and calculus build-up.

By the time dogs are four years old, 75 percent of them have periodontal disease. It is the most common infection in dogs. Yearly examinations by your veterinarian are essential to maintaining your dog's good health. If your veterinarian detects periodontal disease, he or she may recommend a prophylactic cleaning. To do a thorough cleaning, it will be necessary to put your dog under anesthesia. With modern gas anesthetics and

All puppies need to chew as part of their physical and mental development.

Developing good oral habits from the beginning of your puppy's life will keep his teeth healthy and intact.

monitoring equipment, the procedure is pretty safe. Your veterinarian will scale the teeth with an ultrasound scaler or hand instrument. This removes the calculus from the teeth. If there are calculus deposits below the gum line, the veterinarian will plane the roots to make them smooth. After all of the calculus has been removed, the teeth are polished with pumice in a polishing cup. If any medical or surgical treatment is needed, it is done at this time. The final step would be fluoride treatment and your follow-up treatment at home. If the periodontal disease is advanced, the veterinarian may prescribe a medicated mouth rinse or antibiotics for use at home. Make sure your dog has safe, clean and attractive chew toys and treats.

As your dog ages, professional examination and cleaning should become more frequent. The mouth should be inspected at least once a year. Your veterinarian may recommend visits every six months. In the geriatric patient, organs such as the heart, liver, and kidneys do not function as well as when they were young. Your veterinarian will probably want to test these organs' functions prior to using general anesthesia for dental cleaning. If your dog is a good chewer and you work closely with your veterinarian, your dog can keep all of its teeth all of its life. However, as your dog ages, his sense of smell, sight, and taste will diminish. He may not have the desire to chase, trap or chew his toys. He will also not have the energy to chew for long periods, as arthritis and periodontal disease make chewing painful. This will leave you with more responsibility for keeping his teeth clean and healthy. The dog that would not let you brush his teeth at one year of age, may let you brush his teeth now that he is ten years old.

If you train your dog with good chewing habits as a puppy, he will have healthier teeth throughout his life.

TRAVELING with Your Dog

The earlier you start traveling with your new puppy or dog, the better. He needs to become accustomed to traveling. However, some dogs are nervous riders and become carsick easily. It is helpful if he starts with an empty stomach. Do not despair, as it will go better if you continue taking him with you on short fun rides. How would you feel if every time you rode in the car you stopped at the doctor's for an injection? You would soon dread that nasty car. Older dogs that tend to get carsick may have more of a problem adjusting to traveling. Those dogs that are having a serious problem may benefit from some medication prescribed by the veterinarian.

Do give your dog a chance to relieve himself before getting into the car. It is a good idea to be prepared for a clean up with a leash, paper towels, bag and terry cloth towel.

The safest place for your dog is in a fiberglass crate, although close confinement can promote carsickness in some dogs. If your dog is nervous you can try letting him ride on the seat next to you or in someone's lap.

An alternative to the crate would be to use a car harness made for dogs and/or a safety strap attached to the harness or collar. Whatever you do, do

It's a good idea to give your Pug the chance to relieve himself before taking a car trip.

not let your dog ride in the back of a pickup truck unless he is securely tied on a very short lead. I've seen trucks stop quickly and, even though the dog was tied, it fell out and was dragged.

Another advantage of the crate is that it is a safe place to leave him if you need to run into the store. Otherwise you wouldn't be able to leave the windows down. Keep in mind that while many dogs are overly protective in their crates, this may not be enough to deter dognappers. In some states it is against the law to leave a dog in the car unattended.

Never leave a dog loose in the car wearing a collar and leash. More than one dog has killed himself by hanging. Do not let him put his head out an open window. Foreign debris can be blown into his eyes. Never leave your dog in the car in warm weather. It can take less than five minutes to reach temperatures over 100 degrees Fahrenheit.

TRIPS

Perhaps you are taking a trip. Give consideration to what is best for your dog—traveling with you or boarding. When traveling by car, van or motor home, you need to think ahead about locking your vehicle. In all probability you have many valuables in the car and do not wish to leave it unlocked. Perhaps most valuable and not replaceable is your dog. Give thought to securing your vehicle and providing adequate ventilation for him. Another consideration for you when traveling with your dog is medical problems that may arise and little inconveniences, such as exposure to external parasites. Some areas of the country are quite flea infested. You may want to carry flea spray with you. This is even a good idea when staying in motels. Quite possibly you are not the only occupant of the room.

Unbelievably many motels and even hotels do allow canine guests, even some very first-class ones. Gaines Pet Foods Corporation publishes *Touring With Towser*, a directory of domestic hotels and motels that accommodate guests with dogs. Their address is Gaines TWT, PO Box 5700, Kankakee, IL, 60902. Call ahead to any motel that you may be considering and see if they accept pets. Sometimes it is necessary to pay a deposit against room damage. The management may feel reassured if you mention that your dog will be crated. If you do travel with your dog, take along plenty of baggies so that you can clean up after him. When we all do our share in cleaning up, we make it possible for motels

Traveling with your dog requires a lot of preparation. Before embarking on a trip, make sure that your Pug is safe and secure when riding in the car.

to continue accepting our pets. As a matter of fact, you should practice cleaning up everywhere you take your dog.

Depending on where your are traveling, you may need an up-to-date health certificate issued by your veterinarian. It is good policy to take along your dog's medical information, which would include the name, address and phone number of your veterinarian, vaccination record, rabies certificate, and any medication he is taking.

AIR TRAVEL

When traveling by air, you need to contact the airlines to check their policy. Usually you have to make arrangements up to a couple of weeks in advance for traveling with your dog. The airlines require your dog to travel in an airline approved fiberglass crate. Usually these can be purchased through the airlines but they are also readily available in most pet-supply stores. If your dog is not accustomed to a crate, then it is a good idea to get him acclimated to it before your trip. The day of the actual trip you should withhold water about one hour ahead of departure and no food for about 12 hours. The airlines generally have temperature restrictions, which do not allow pets to travel if it is either too cold or too hot. Frequently these restrictions are based on the temperatures at the departure and arrival airports. It's best to inquire about a health certificate. These usually need to be issued within ten days of departure. You should arrange for non-stop, direct flights and if a commuter plane should be involved, check to see if it will carry dogs. Some don't. The Humane Society of the United States has put together a tip sheet for airline traveling. You can receive a copy by sending a self-addressed stamped envelope to:

The Humane Society of the United States
Tip Sheet
2100 L Street NW
Washington, DC 20037.

Regulations differ for traveling outside of the country and are sometimes changed without notice. Well in advance you need to write or call the appropriate consulate or agricultural department for instructions. Some countries have lengthy quarantines (six months), and countries differ in their rabies vaccination requirements. For instance, it may have to be given at least 30 days ahead of your departure.

Do make sure your dog is wearing proper identification including your name, phone number and city. You never know when you might be in an accident and separated from your dog. Or your dog could be frightened and somehow manage to escape and run away.

Another suggestion would be to carry in-case-of-emergency instructions. These would include the address and phone number of a relative or friend, your veterinarian's name, address and phone number, and your dog's medical information.

BOARDING KENNELS

Perhaps you have decided that you need to board your dog. Your veterinarian can recommend a good boarding facility or possibly a pet sitter that will come to your house. It is customary for the boarding kennel to ask for proof of vaccination for the DHLPP, rabies and bordetella vaccine. The bordetella should have been given within six months of boarding. This is for your protection. If they do not ask for this proof I would not board at

Before putting your Pug in a boarding kennel, visit the facilities to make sure that they are clean and run efficiently.

their kennel. Ask about flea control. Those dogs that suffer flea-bite allergy can get in trouble at a boarding kennel. Unfortunately boarding kennels are limited on how much they are able to do.

For more information on pet sitting, contact NAPPS:
National Association of Professional Pet Sitters
1200 G Street, NW
Suite 760
Washington, DC 20005.

Some pet clinics have technicians that pet sit and technicians that board clinic patients in their homes. This may be an alternative for you. Ask your veterinarian if they have an employee that can help you. There is a definite advantage of having a technician care for your dog, especially if your dog is on medication or is a senior citizen.

You can write for a copy of *Traveling With Your Pet* from ASPCA, Education Department, 441 E. 92nd Street, New York, NY 10128.

IDENTIFICATION and Finding the Lost Dog

There are several ways of identifying your dog. The old standby is a collar with dog license, rabies, and ID tags. Unfortunately collars have a way of being separated from the dog and tags fall off. We're not suggesting you shouldn't use a collar and tags. If they stay intact and on the dog, they are the quickest way of identification.

For several years owners have been tattooing their dogs. Some tattoos use a number with a registry. Here lies the problem because there are several registries to check. If you wish to tattoo, use your social security number. The humane shelters have the means to trace it. It is usually done on the inside of the rear thigh. The area is first shaved and numbed. There is no pain, although a few dogs do not like the buzzing sound. Occasionally tattooing is not legible and needs to be redone.

The newest method of identification is microchipping. The microchip is a computer chip that is no larger than a grain of rice. The veterinarian implants it by injection between the shoulder blades. The dog feels no discomfort. If your dog is lost and picked up by the humane society, they can trace you by scanning the

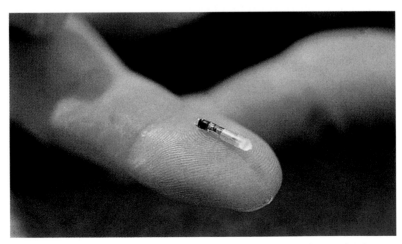

The newest method of identification is the microchip, which is a chip no bigger than a grain of rice that will help you track your dog's whereabouts.

An exercise pen is a safe and humane way to contain your Pug while you are away from home.

microchip, which has its own code. Microchip scanners are friendly to other brands of microchips and their registries. The microchip comes with a dog tag saying the dog is microchipped. It is the safest way of identifying your dog.

FINDING THE LOST DOG

I am sure you will agree that there would be little worse than losing your dog. Responsible pet owners rarely lose their dogs. They do not let their dogs run free because they don't want harm to come to them. Not only that but in most, if not all, states there is a leash law.

Beware of fenced-in yards. They can be a hazard. Dogs find ways to escape either over or under the fence. Another fast exit is through the gate that perhaps the neighbor's child left unlocked.

Below is a list that hopefully will be of help to you if you need it. Remember don't give up, keep looking. Your dog is worth your efforts.

1. Contact your neighbors and put flyers with a photo on it in their mailboxes. Information you should include would be the dog's name, breed, sex, color, age, source of identification, when your dog was last seen and where, and your name and phone numbers. It may be helpful to say the dog needs medical care. Offer a *reward*.

2. Check all local shelters daily. It is also possible for your dog to be picked up away from home and end up in an out-of-the-way shelter. Check these too. Go in person. It is not good enough to call. Most shelters are limited on the time they can hold dogs then they are put up for adoption or euthanized. There is the possibility that your dog will not make it to the shelter for several days. Your dog could have been wandering or someone may have tried to keep him.

3. Notify all local veterinarians. Call and send flyers.

4. Call your breeder. Frequently breeders are contacted when one of their breed is found.

5. Contact the rescue group for your breed.

6. Contact local schools—children may have seen your dog.

7. Post flyers at the schools, groceries, gas stations, convenience stores, veterinary clinics, groomers and any other place that will allow them.

8. Advertise in the newspaper.

9. Advertise on the radio.

BEHAVIOR and Canine Communication

Studies of the human/animal bond point out the importance of the unique relationships that exist between people and their pets. Those of us who share our lives with pets understand the special part they play through companionship, service and protection. For many, the pet/owner bond goes beyond simple companionship; pets are often considered members of the family. A leading pet food manufacturer recently conducted a nationwide survey of pet owners to gauge just how important pets were in their lives. Here's what they found:

- 76 percent allow their pets to sleep on their beds
- 78 percent think of their pets as their children
- 84 percent display photos of their pets, mostly in their homes
- 84 percent think that their pets react to their own emotions
- 100 percent talk to their pets
- 97 percent think that their pets understand what they're saying

Are you surprised?

Senior citizens show more concern for their own eating habits when they have the responsibility of feeding a dog. Seeing that their dog is routinely exercised encourages the owner to think of schedules that otherwise may seem unimportant to the senior citizen. The older owner may be arthritic and feeling poorly but with responsibility for his dog he has a reason to get up and get moving. It is a big plus if his dog is an attention seeker who will demand such from his owner.

Over the last couple of decades, it has been shown that pets relieve the stress of those who lead busy lives. Owning a pet has been known to lessen the occurrence of heart attack and stroke.

Many single folks thrive on the companionship of a dog. Lifestyles are very different from a long time ago, and today more individuals seek the single life. However, they receive fulfillment from owning a dog.

Most likely the majority of our dogs live in family environments. The companionship they provide is well worth the effort involved. In my opinion, every child should have the opportunity to have a family dog. Dogs teach responsibility through understanding their care, feelings and even respecting their life cycles. Frequently those children who have not been exposed to dogs grow up afraid

Having your child take part in caring for the family dog is a good lesson in responsibility. It also helps a child to feel comfortable and secure around animals.

of dogs, which isn't good. Dogs sense timidity and some will take advantage of the situation.

Today more dogs are serving as service dogs. Since the origination of the Seeing Eye dogs years ago, we now have trained hearing dogs. Also dogs are trained to provide service for the handicapped and are able to perform many different tasks for their owners. Search and Rescue dogs, with their handlers, are sent throughout the world to assist in recovery of disaster victims. They are life savers.

Therapy dogs are very popular with nursing homes, and some hospitals even allow them to visit. The inhabitants truly look forward to their visits. They wanted and were allowed to have visiting dogs in their beds to hold and love.

Nationally there is a Pet Awareness Week to educate students and others about the value and basic care of our pets. Many countries take an even greater interest in their pets than Americans do. In those countries the pets are allowed to accompany their owners into restaurants and shops, etc. In the U.S. this freedom is only available to our service dogs. Even so we think very highly of the human/animal bond.

CANINE BEHAVIOR

Canine behavior problems are the number-one reason for pet owners to dispose of their dogs, either through new homes, humane shelters or euthanasia. Unfortunately there are too many owners who are unwilling to devote the necessary time to properly train their dogs. On the other hand, there are those who not only are concerned about inherited health problems but are also aware of the dog's mental stability.

You may realize that a breed and his group relatives (i.e., sporting, hounds, etc.) show tendencies to behavioral characteristics. An experienced breeder can acquaint you with his breed's personality. Unfortunately many breeds are labeled with poor temperaments when actually the breed as a whole is not affected but only a small percentage of individuals within the breed.

Inheritance and environment contribute to the dog's behavior. Some naïve people suggest inbreeding as the cause of bad temperaments. Inbreeding only results in poor behavior if the ancestors carry the trait. If there are excellent temperaments behind the dogs, then inbreeding will promote good temperaments

Although a busy schedule can make spending time with your dog difficult, make sure that he has adequate mental and physical stimulation to keep him healthy and happy.

in the offspring. Did you ever consider that inbreeding is what sets the characteristics of a breed? A purebred dog is the end result of inbreeding. This does not spare the mixed-breed dog from the same problems. Mixed-breed dogs frequently are the offspring of purebred dogs.

Not too many decades ago most of our dogs led a different lifestyle than what is prevalent today. Usually mom stayed home so the dog had human companionship and someone to discipline it if needed. Not much was expected from the dog. Today's mom works and everyone's life is at a much faster pace.

The dog may have to adjust to being a "weekend" dog. The family is gone all day during the week, and the dog is left to his own devices for entertainment. Some dogs sleep all day waiting for their family to come home and others become wigwam wreckers if given the opportunity. Crates do ensure the safety of the dog and the house. However, he could become a physically and emotionally cripple if he doesn't get enough exercise and attention. We still appreciate and want the companionship of our dogs although we expect more from them. In many cases we tend to forget dogs are just that—*dogs*—not human beings.

SOCIALIZING AND TRAINING

Many prospective puppy buyers lack experience regarding the proper socialization and training needed to develop the type of pet we all desire. In the first 18 months, training does take some work. It is easier to start proper training before there is a problem that needs to be corrected.

The initial work begins with the breeder. The breeder should start socializing the puppy at five to six weeks of age and cannot let up. Human socializing is critical up through 12 weeks of age and likewise important during the following months. The litter should be left together during the first few weeks but it is necessary to separate them by ten weeks of age. Leaving them together after that time will increase competition for litter dominance. If puppies are not socialized with people by 12 weeks of age, they will be timid in later life.

The eight- to ten-week age period is a fearful time for puppies. They need to be handled very gently around children and adults. There should be no harsh discipline during this time. Starting at 14 weeks of age, the puppy begins the juvenile period, which ends when he reaches sexual maturity around six to 14 months of age. During the juvenile period he needs to be introduced to strangers (adults, children and other dogs) on the home property. At sexual maturity he will begin to bark at strangers and become

Socialization with his dam and littermates will help your Pug get along with other dogs when he is older.

more protective. Males start to lift their legs to urinate but if you desire you can inhibit this behavior by walking your boy on leash away from trees, shrubs, fences, etc.

Perhaps you are thinking about an older puppy. You need to inquire about the puppy's social experience. If he has lived in a kennel, he may have a hard time adjusting to people and environmental stimuli. Assuming he has had a good social upbringing, there are advantages to an older puppy.

Training includes puppy kindergarten and a minimum of one to two basic training classes. During these classes you will learn how to dominate your youngster. This is especially important if you own a large breed of dog. It is somewhat harder, if not nearly impossible, for some owners to be the Alpha figure when their dog towers over them. You will be taught how to properly restrain your dog. This concept is important. Again it puts you in the Alpha position. All dogs need to be restrained many times during their lives. Believe it or not, some of our worst offenders are the eight-week-old puppies that are brought to our clinic. They need to be gently restrained for a nail trim but the way they carry on you would think we were killing them. In comparison, their vaccination is a "piece of cake." When we ask dogs to do something that is not agreeable to them, then their worst comes out. Life will be easier for your dog if you expose him at a young age to the necessities of life—proper behavior and restraint.

UNDERSTANDING THE DOG'S LANGUAGE

Most authorities agree that the dog is a descendent of the wolf. The dog and wolf have similar traits. For instance both are pack oriented and prefer not to be isolated for long periods of time. Another characteristic is that the dog, like the wolf, looks to the leader—Alpha—for direction. Both the wolf and the dog communicate through body language, not only within their pack but with outsiders.

Every pack has an Alpha figure. The dog looks to you, or should look to you, to be that leader. If your dog doesn't receive the proper training and guidance, he very well may replace you as Alpha. This would be a serious problem and is certainly a disservice to your dog.

Eye contact is one way the Alpha wolf keeps order within his pack. You are Alpha so you must establish eye contact with your puppy. Obviously your puppy will have to look at you. Practice eye contact even if you need to hold his head for five to ten seconds at a time. You can give him a treat as a reward. Make sure your eye contact is gentle and not threatening. Later, if he has been naughty, it is permissible to give him a long, penetrating look. There are some older dogs that never learned eye contact as puppies and cannot accept eye contact. You should avoid eye contact with these dogs since they feel threatened and will retaliate as such.

Your Pug should look to you as his Alpha, or pack leader. Establishing gentle eye contact with him will let him know that you are in charge.

Body Language

The play bow, when the forequarters are down and the hindquarters are elevated, is an invitation to play. Puppies play fight, which helps them learn the acceptable limits of biting. This is necessary for later in their lives. Nevertheless, an owner may be falsely reassured by the playful nature of his dog's aggression. Playful aggression toward another dog or human may be an indication of serious aggression in the future. Owners should never play fight or play tug-of-war with any dog that is inclined to be dominant.

Signs of submission are:

1. Avoids eye contact.

2. Active submission—the dog crouches down, ears back and the tail is lowered.

3. Passive submission—the dog rolls on his side with his hindlegs in the air and frequently urinates.

Signs of dominance are:

1. Makes eye contact.

Your dog's body language can tell you how he is feeling in certain situations. Peepers lets his two buddies, Chumby and Duke, know that size doesn't matter.

    2. Stands with ears up, tail up and the hair raised on his neck.

    3. Shows dominance over another dog by standing at right angles over it.

Dominant dogs tend to behave in characteristic ways such as:

    1. The dog may be unwilling to move from his place (i.e., reluctant to give up the sofa if the owner wants to sit there).

    2. He may not part with toys or objects in his mouth and may show possessiveness with his food bowl.

    3. He may not respond quickly to commands.

    4. He may be disagreeable for grooming and dislikes to be petted.

Dogs are popular because of their sociable nature. Those that have contact with humans during the first 12 weeks of life regard them as a member of their own species—their pack. All dogs have the potential for both dominant and submissive behavior. Only through experience and training do they learn to whom it is appropriate to show which behavior. Not all dogs are concerned with dominance but owners need to be aware of that potential. It is wise for the owner to establish his dominance early on.

A human can express dominance or submission toward a dog in the following ways:

1. Meeting the dog's gaze signals dominance. Averting the gaze signals submission. If the dog growls or threatens, averting the gaze is the first avoiding action to take—it may prevent attack. It is important to establish eye contact in the puppy. The older dog that has not been exposed to eye contact may see it as a threat and will not be willing to submit.

2. Being taller than the dog signals dominance; being lower signals submission. This is why, when attempting to make friends with a strange dog or catch the runaway, one should kneel down to his level. Some owners see their dogs become dominant when allowed on the furniture or on the bed. Then he is at the owner's level.

3. An owner can gain dominance by ignoring all the dog's social initiatives. The owner pays attention to the dog only when he obeys a command.

No dog should be allowed to achieve dominant status over any adult or child. Ways of preventing are as follows:

1. Handle the puppy gently, especially during the three- to four-month period.

2. Let the children and adults handfeed him and teach him to take food without lunging or grabbing.

3. Do not allow him to chase children or joggers.

4. Do not allow him to jump on people or mount their legs. Even females may be inclined to mount. It is not only a male habit.

5. Do not allow him to growl for any reason.

6. Don't participate in wrestling or tug-of-war games.

7. Don't physically punish puppies for aggressive behavior. Restrain him from repeating the infraction and teach an alternative behavior. Dogs should earn everything they receive from their owners. This would include sitting to receive petting or treats, sitting before going out the door and sitting to receive the collar and leash. These types of exercises reinforce the owner's dominance.

Young children should never be left alone with a dog. It is important that children learn some basic obedience commands so they have some control over the dog. They will gain the respect of their dog.

Your Pug may display a fear of new things or situations. Be patient and give him time to get used to unfamiliar things.

FEAR

One of the most common problems dogs experience is being fearful. Some dogs are more afraid than others. On the lesser side, which is sometimes humorous to watch, dogs can be afraid of a strange object. They act silly when something is out of place in the house. We call his problem perceptive intelligence. He realizes the abnormal within his known environment. He does not react the same way in strange environments since he does not know what is normal.

On the more serious side is a fear of people. This can result in backing off, seeking his own space and saying "leave me alone" or it can result in an aggressive behavior that may lead to challenging the person. Respect that the dog wants to be left alone and give him time to come forward. If you approach the cornered dog, he may resort to snapping. If you leave him alone, he may decide to come forward, which should be rewarded with a treat.

Some dogs may initially be too fearful to take treats. In these cases it is helpful to make sure the dog hasn't eaten for about 24 hours. Being a little hungry encourages him to accept the treats, especially if they are of the "gourmet" variety.

Dogs can be afraid of numerous things, including loud noises and thunderstorms. Invariably the owner rewards (by comforting) the dog when it shows signs of fearfulness. When your dog is frightened, direct his attention to something else and act happy. Don't dwell on his fright.

AGGRESSION

Some different types of aggression are: predatory, defensive, dominance, possessive, protective, fear induced, noise provoked, "rage" syndrome (unprovoked aggression), maternal and aggression directed toward other dogs. Aggression is the most common behavioral problem encountered. Protective breeds are expected to be more aggressive than others but with the proper upbringing they can make very dependable companions. You need to be able to read your dog.

Many factors contribute to aggression including genetics and environment. An improper environment, which may include the living conditions, lack of social life, excessive punishment, being attacked or frightened by an aggressive dog, etc., can all influence a dog's behavior. Even spoiling him and giving too much praise may be detrimental. Isolation and the lack of human contact or exposure to frequent teasing by children or adults also can ruin a good dog.

Lack of direction, fear, or confusion lead to aggression in those dogs that are so inclined. Any obedience exercise, even

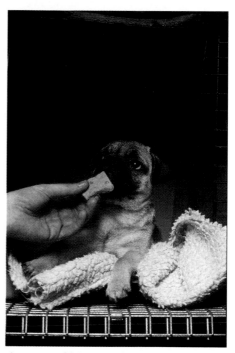

As part of his socialization training, your Pug should learn to accept foods and treats without displaying aggression.

the sit and down, can direct the dog and overcome fear and/or confusion. Every dog should learn these commands as a youngster, and there should be periodic reinforcement.

When a dog is showing signs of aggression, you should speak calmly (no screaming or hysterics) and firmly give a command that he understands, such as the sit. As soon as your dog obeys, you have assumed your dominant position. Aggression presents a problem because there may be danger to others. Sometimes it is an emotional issue. Owners may consciously or unconsciously encourage their dog's aggression. Other owners show responsibility by accepting the problem and taking measures to keep it under control. The owner is responsible for his dog's actions, and it is not wise to take a chance on someone being bitten, especially a child. Euthanasia is the solution for some owners and in severe cases this may be the best choice. However, few dogs are that dangerous and very few are that much of a threat to their owners. If caution is exercised and professional help is gained early on, most cases can be controlled.

Some authorities recommend feeding a lower protein (less than 20 percent) diet. They believe this can aid in reducing aggression. If the dog loses weight, then vegetable oil can be added. Veterinarians and behaviorists are having some success with pharmacology. In many cases treatment is possible and can improve the situation.

If you have done everything according to "the book" regarding training and socializing and are still having a behavior problem, don't procrastinate. It is important that the problem gets attention before it is out of hand. It is estimated that 20 percent of a veterinarian's time may be devoted to dealing with problems before they become so intolerable that the dog is separated from its home and owner. If your veterinarian isn't able to help, he should refer you to a behaviorist.

Problems

Barking

This is a habit that shouldn't be encouraged. Some owners desire their dog to bark so as to be a watchdog. Most dogs will bark when a stranger comes to the door.

The new puppy frequently barks or whines in the crate in his strange environment and the owner reinforces the puppy's bad

With the proper socialization and training, your Pug will become an enjoyable companion and good canine citizen.

behavior by going to him during the night. This is a no-no. Smack the top of the crate and say "quiet" in a loud, firm voice. The puppies don't like to hear the loud noise of the crate being banged. If the barking is sleep-interrupting, then the owner should take crate and pup to the bedroom for a few days until the puppy becomes adjusted to his new environment. Otherwise ignore the barking during the night.

Barking can be an inherited problem or a bad habit learned through the environment. It takes dedication to stop the barking. Attention should be paid to the cause of the barking. Does the dog seek attention, does he need to go out, is it feeding time, is it occurring when he is left alone, is it a protective bark, etc.? Overzealous barking is an inherited tendency. When barking presents a problem for you, try to stop it as soon as it begins.

There are electronic collars available that are supposed to curb barking. There are some disadvantages to to the collar. If the dog is barking out of excitement, punishment is not the appropriate treatment. Presumably there is the chance the collar could be activated by other stimuli and thereby punish the dog when it is not barking. Should you decide to use one, then you should seek help from a person with experience with that type of collar.

Nevertheless the root of the problem needs to be investigated and corrected.

In extreme circumstances (usually when there is a problem with the neighbors), some people have resorted to having their dogs debarked. I caution you that the dog continues to bark but usually only a squeaking sound is heard. Frequently the vocal cords grow back. Probably the biggest concern is that the dog can be left with scar tissue which can narrow the opening to the trachea.

Jumping Up

A dog that jumps up is a happy dog. Nevertheless few guests appreciate dogs jumping on them. Clothes get footprinted and/or snagged.

Some trainers believe in allowing the puppy to jump up during his first few weeks. If you correct him too soon and at the wrong age you may intimidate him. Consequently he could be timid around humans later in his life. However, there will come a time, probably around four months of age, that he needs to know when it is okay to jump and when he is to show off good manners by sitting instead.

Some authorities never allow jumping. If you are irritated by your dog jumping up on you, then you should discourage it from the beginning. A larger breed of dog can cause harm to a senior citizen. Some are quite fragile. It may not take much to cause a topple that could break a hip.

How do you correct the problem? All family members need to participate in teaching the puppy to sit as soon as he starts to jump up. The sit must be practiced every time he starts to jump up. Don't forget to praise him for his good behavior. If an older dog has acquired the habit, grasp his paws and squeeze tightly. Give a firm "No." He'll soon catch on. Remember the entire family must take part. Each time you allow him to jump up you go back a step in training.

Biting

All puppies bite and try to chew on your fingers, toes, arms, etc. This is the time to teach them to be gentle and not bite hard. Put your fingers in your puppy's mouth and if he bites too hard then say "easy" and let him know he's hurting you. Squeal and act like you have been seriously hurt. If the puppy plays too rough and

Occasionally, puppies may tend to show improper behavior such as biting or barking. Correct these behaviors by using firm but positive reinforcement.

doesn't respond to your corrections, then he needs "Time Out" in his crate. You should be particularly careful with young children and puppies who still have their deciduous (baby) teeth. Those teeth are like needles and can leave little scars on youngsters.

Biting in the more mature dog is something that should be prevented at all costs. Should it occur quickly let him know in no uncertain terms that biting will not be tolerated. When biting is directed toward another dog (dog fight), don't get in the middle of it. Some authorities recommend breaking up a fight by elevating the hind legs. This would only be possible if there was a person for each dog. Obviously it would be hard to fight with the hind legs off the ground. A dog bite is serious and should be given attention. Wash the bite with soap and water and contact your doctor. It is important to know the status of the offender's rabies vaccination.

Your dog must know who is boss. When biting occurs, you should seek professional help at once. On the other hand you must not let your dog intimidate you and be so afraid of a bite that you can't discipline him. Professional help through your veterinarian, dog trainer and/or behaviorist can give you guidance.

There are many factors that contribute to a pet's happiness, such as a healthy living environment, good care, and unconditional love.

Digging

Bored dogs release their frustrations through mischievous behavior such as digging. Dogs shouldn't be left unattended outside, even if they are in a fenced-in yard. Usually the dog is sent to "jail" (the backyard) because the owner can't tolerate him in the house. The culprit feels socially deprived and needs to be included in the owner's life. The owner has neglected the dog's training. The dog has not developed into the companion we desire. If you are one of these owners, then perhaps it is possible for you to change. Give him another chance. Some owners object to their dog's unkempt coat and doggy odor. See that he is groomed on a regular schedule and look into some training classes.

Submissive Urination

This is not a housebreaking problem. It can occur in all breeds and may be more prevalent in some breeds. Usually it occurs in puppies but occasionally it occurs in older dogs and may be in response to physical praise. Try verbal praise or ignoring your dog until after he has had a chance to relieve himself. Scolding will only make the problem worse. Many dogs outgrow this problem.

Misbehavior is a sure sign of boredom. Provide your Pug with enough activities to keep him occupied.

Coprophagia

Also know as stool eating, sometimes occurs without a cause. It may begin with boredom and then becomes a habit that is hard to break. Your best remedy is to keep the puppy on a leash and keep the yard picked up. Then he won't have an opportunity to get in trouble. Your veterinarian can dispense a medication that is put on the dog's food that makes the stool taste bitter. Of course this will do little good if your dog cleans up after other dogs.

The Runaway

There is little excuse for a dog to run away since dogs should never be off leash except when supervised in the fenced-in yard.

Many prospective owners that want to purchase a female since a male is inclined to roam. It is true that an intact male is inclined to roam, which is one of the reasons a male should be neutered. However, females will roam also, especially if they are in heat. Regardless, these dogs should never be given this opportunity. A few years ago one of our clients elected euthanasia for her elderly dog that radiographically appeared to have an intestinal blockage. The veterinarian suggested it might be a corncob. She assured him that was not possible since they hadn't had any. Apparently he roamed and raided the neighbor's garbage and you guessed it—he had a corncob blocking his intestines. Another dog raided the neighbor's garbage and died from toxins from the garbage.

To give the benefit of the doubt, perhaps your dog escapes or perhaps you are playing with your dog in the yard and he refuses to come when called. You now have a runaway. Help! The first thing to remember is when you finally do catch your naughty dog, you must not discipline him. The reasoning behind this is that it is quite possible there could be a repeat performance, and it would be nice if the next time he would respond to your sweet command.

Always kneel down when trying to catch the runaway. Dogs are afraid of people standing over them. Also it would be helpful to have a treat or a favorite toy to help entice him to your side. After that initial runaway experience, start practicing the recall with your dog. You can let him drag a long line (clothesline) and randomly call him and then reel him in. Let him touch you first. Reaching for the dog can frighten him. Each time he comes you reward him with a treat and eventually he should get the idea that this is a nice experience. The long line prevents him from really

Feed your puppy in a relaxing area without the presence of children or other pets, which could interfere with his eating.

Provide your dog with enough physical activity and attention to prevent him from getting into mischief.

getting out of hand. At least with the long line you can step on it and stop him.

Food Guarding

If you see signs of your puppy guarding his food, then you should take immediate steps to correct the problem. It is not fair to your puppy to feed him in a busy environment where children or other pets may interfere with his eating. This can be the cause of food guarding. Puppies should be fed in their crates where they do not feel threatened. Another advantage of this is that the puppy gets down to the business of eating and doesn't fool around. Perhaps you have seen possessiveness over the food bowl or his toys. Start by feeding him out of your hand and teach him that it is okay for you to remove his food bowl or toy and that you most assuredly will return it to him. If your dog is truly a bad actor and intimidates you, try keeping him on leash and perhaps sit next to him making happy talk. At feeding time make him work for his reward (his dinner) by doing some obedience command such as sit or down. Before your problem gets out of control you should get professional help. If he is out of control over toys, perhaps you should dispose of them or at least put them away when young children are around.

Mischief and Misbehavior

All puppies and even some adult dogs will get into mischief at some time in their lives. You should start by "puppy proofing" your house. Even so it is impossible to have a sterile environment.

For instance, if you would be down to four walls and a floor your dog could still chew a hole in the wall. What do you do? Remember puppies should never be left unsupervised so let us go on to the trusted adult dog that has misbehaved. His behavior may be an attention getter. Dogs, and even children, are known to do mischief even though they know they will be punished. Your puppy/dog will benefit from more attention and new direction. He may benefit from a training class or by reinforcing the obedience he has already learned. How about a daily walk? That could be a good outlet for your dog, time together and exercise for both of you.

Separation Anxiety

This occurs when dogs feel distress or apprehension when separated from their owners. One of the mistakes owners make is to set their dogs up for their departure. Some authorities recommend paying little attention to the pet for at least ten minutes before leaving and for the first ten minutes after you arrive home. The dog isn't cued to the fact you are leaving and if

If your dog is having anxiety about being left alone, try leaving him for just a few minutes at a time, then returning and rewarding him with a treat.

you keep it lowkey they learn to accept it as a normal everyday occurrence. Those dogs that are used to being crated usually accept your departure. Dogs that are anxious may have a serious problem and wreak havoc on the house within a few minutes after your departure. You can try to acclimate your dog to the separation by leaving for just a few minutes at a time, returning and rewarding him with a treat. Don't get too carried away. Plan on this process taking a long time. A behaviorist can set down a schedule for you. Those dogs that are insecure, such as ones obtained from a humane shelter or those that have changed homes, present more of a problem.

Punishment

A puppy should learn that correction is sometimes necessary and should not question your authority. An older dog that has never received correction may retaliate. In my opinion there will be a time for physical punishment but this does not mean hitting the dog. Do not use newspapers, fly swatters, etc. One type of correction, that is used by the mother dog when she corrects her puppies, is to take the puppy by the scruff and shake him *gently*. For the older, larger dog you can grab the scruff, one hand on each side of his neck, and lift his legs off the ground. This is effective since dogs feel intimidated when their feet are off the ground. Timing is of the utmost importance when punishment is necessary. Depending on the degree of fault, you might want to reinforce punishment by ignoring your dog for 15 to 20 minutes. Whatever you do, do not overdo corrections or they will lose value.

The most important advice to you is to be aware of your dog's actions. Even so, remember dogs are dogs and will behave as such even though we might like them to be perfect little people. You and your dog will become neurotic if you worry about every little indiscretion. When there is reason for concern—don't waste time. Seek guidance. Dogs are meant to be loved and enjoyed.

References:

Manual of Canine Behavior, Valerie O'Farrell, British Small Animal Veterinary Association.

Good Owners, Great Dogs, Brian Kilcommons, Warner Books.

INDEX

PHOTO CREDITS